MONEY $MART MOM

*Financially Fit
Parenting*

Sarah Deveau

Cater Tot Publishing, Airdrie, Alberta

Cater Tot Publishing
29 Spring Haven Cresent
Airdrie, Alberta, Canada T4A 1A7
www.moneysmartmom.ca
403 • 420 • 1727

First Paperback Edition – May 2010
15 14 13 12 11 10 — 1 2 3 4 5 6 7 8 9 10

Library and Archives Canada Cataloguing in Publication

Deveau, Sarah
    Money $mart mom: financially fit parenting / Sarah Deveau. 1st. pbk. ed.

Includes bibliographic references and index.
ISBN 978–0–9865415–0–6

1. Parents—Finance, Personal. 2. Parenting. 3. Child rearing—Economic aspects. 4. Families—Economic aspects. I. Title. II. Title: Money smart mom.

    HG179.D4946 2010   332.0240085   C2010-901958-X

The article entitled *Still No Emergency Fund? Really?* on pages 69 – 71 of this book is reprinted by permission of its author and remains the copyright of Gail Vaz-Oxlade.

Technical Credits:
Editing: Elizabeth Groskorth, Mississauga, Ontario
Proofreading and index: Natalie Boon, *Boon Information Services*, Toronto, Ontario
Final editing, design and production: Jeremy Drought, *Last Impression Publishing Service*, Calgary, Alberta
Front cover image: Kristen Shima, *Shima Studios*, Airdrie, Alberta
Back cover image of author: Michelle Moores, Airdrie, Aberta
Printed in Canada by *Marquis Impimeur Inc.*, Montréal, Québec

Acknowledgements

I'D LIKE TO THANK THE many Money Smart Moms (and dads too!) who took the time to be candid with me about their finances, and contributed tips and stories. Thank you to my many early readers, especially Joan Bell and Lisa Sierra. Your insights were invaluable. A big thank you to Jeremy Drought for your patience and wisdom in helping me polish this book and get it into bookstores.

Thanks to my three girls for being good sleepers! Your long naps and early bedtimes made it possible for me to write down all the advice I found myself repeating endlessly at playgroups.

For Kate, Jacqueline, and Nicole.

Contents

Introduction:
What to Expect from this Book

YOU MIGHT HAVE PICKED UP this book because you're thinking about having kids and you have no idea how you'll ever be able to afford it. You might have kids already and don't understand why you're still living paycheque to paycheque like you did in college. Perhaps someone gave you this book as a gift. Whether you have kids yet or are still in the planning stages, are in debt up to your eyeballs or just barely keeping up, this book can help.

For some families, this book will provide them with the information they need to dig out of their debt, enabling them more freedom in their financial decision making. For others, it will help them manage having a one-income household. It might provide enough information to guide families in finding the extra money to contribute to an RESP. It may give others strategies for handling money without fighting, even if their earning, spending and saving doesn't change a nickel.

What you get out of this book will depend on your particular situation, and how you want to approach your finances. I can't give you one perfect way to raise kids without being or feeling financially strapped, but I can provide you with the tools you need to make the best decisions for you and your family.

For instance, I can tell you that cloth diapers will save you hundreds of dollars per child over disposables, but if you don't have a washing machine and dryer in your home, if you're squeamish, or you're feeling overwhelmed by all of the responsibilities of being a new parent already, the advice won't be particularly useful to you.

This book will offer not only practical tips, tricks, and advice, but also new ways to look at your personal views on shopping, saving, ownership, and more.

Your job is to challenge your preconceived notions of what you can do, should do, and won't do, then embrace the elements of the book that will work for you, and ignore what won't.

Now, let me preface this by admitting that I'm not perfect (gasp!). I have fallen prey to marketing ploys to spend $100 now on overpriced clothing to earn $50 in "bucks" I can redeem later on more overpriced clothing. I have convinced myself that I "deserved" something I had to put on credit.

I think this is exactly what makes me qualified to help you! I'm a real person who has made financial mistakes, and learned from them. I don't find spending wisely super easy—I track my spending every day to stay on track. Figuring out the right decisions is a constant struggle.

This book includes quotes from other parents in different financial situations; those who did and did not wait until they "had it all" financially, single parents, working parents, and many stay-at-home parents.

If you're reading this and you're male, you've likely noticed the obvious gender bias. I have tried to stay as gender-neutral as possible. However, even when both partners work full time outside of the home, the majority of the time the women do make the buying decisions, and usually have the biggest impact on the family budget. So while this book is called *Money Smart Mom*, the information contained within this book absolutely applies to money smart dads too. I've searched for comments from fathers to include, but the moms were much more likely to open up than the dads, especially about when things were not going the way they had hoped.

I really dislike self-help books that provide readers with one way to live their lives—play by the author's rules, or you'll fail. They don't allow for exceptions in personal circumstances, unforeseeable setbacks, or personal preferences. The reality is—both in dieting and finance—you need to incorporate new habits in ways that reflect your real life or the changes won't stick.

So this is not a tough love book. I'm not going to berate you for being in debt, or call you stupid if you put a third black winter jacket on your credit card. You're an adult, and taking responsibility for your decisions is part and parcel of adulthood. No one will get your finances in order for you. You can hire someone to help or advise you, but eventually they'll be gone and it will be 100% your responsibility again.

After reading this book if you want a more generalized book about debt management that does give you a kick in the pants, I highly recommend either *Debt-Free Forever* by Gail Vaz-Oxlade or *You're Broke Because You Want to Be* by Larry Winget.

A Little Background

In the summer of 2004, my husband, Keith, and I were thinking about having kids. I looked for books about the impact children would have on our finances, but didn't find much, and most of what I did find was written for an American audience. Though there were one or two slim Canadian titles, they just didn't have the practical advice I was looking for. I definitely wasn't interested in reading the preachy advice of someone who had kids twenty years ago, before entire stores were dedicated to designer baby duds, when eight-year-olds preferred a new bike over a video game system, and before ten-year-olds had cell phones. I especially didn't want to read a "my way is the only way" kind of book—I was looking for something that provided options for different scenarios. What good was a book to me if the author considered travelling an unnecessary expense when we considered family travel one of the ultimate joys of life?

So I decided to write the book I wished I had been able to buy at the bookstore. Or rather, write the book I wished I could have borrowed from the library! During this time, our first daughter, Kate, was born in May of 2005. Jacqueline came along in February of 2008, and Nicole followed in September of 2009.

Sarah Deveau
Airdrie, Alberta
March, 2010

CHAPTER ONE

Making the Decision

CCORDING TO A SURVEY CONDUCTED by the Food and Rural Initiatives at Manitoba Agriculture, in 2004 the cost of raising a boy from birth to age 18 was $166,971. Girls cost slightly less, a total of $166,549. Of course, you knew having kids wasn't going to be cheap, but I bet you didn't think they'd be quite that expensive either.

This survey gives estimates on what everything will cost year by year. For example, they estimate clothing a one-year-old girl will cost $515 annually; recreation, reading, gifts and school needs for an 11-year-old boy will run you $794. These costs are based on minimums and averages—they don't reflect the cost of educational savings, putting three boys through minor hockey, dance lessons for two girls, tutoring for a slow learner, or special therapy for a disabled child.

These costs also don't factor in the frugality of a determined parent. A mom who breastfeeds, then prepares her own baby food, will spend just a few hundred dollars annually on a child's food bill. A dad who locates hand-me-downs for all of his infant's needs may only spend $150 on clothing until the child is old enough to start demanding more stylish clothing (not that you have to give in to the demands—more on this in Chapter 10). Planning on having more than one child? Even if they aren't the same gender, subsequent children won't cost nearly as much as the first. Finally, your lifestyle will change significantly when you have children, and this isn't accounted for at all in the charts. Whether you once spent vacations in Hawaii, enjoyed fine restaurants weekly, or even just took in the occasional movie at a first-run theatre, many of these things won't hold as much appeal. Once there are young children in the house, your spending on entertainment, clothing, holidays, and other items for yourself will decrease considerably, freeing up extra dollars to go toward gymnastics lessons, baseball uniforms, and more.

Unfortunately, this study hasn't been updated in six years. However, Edmonton blogger Tom Drake has provided an update to the table taking inflation into account. You can see his post at <**www.canadianfinance blog.com/2009/10/13/how-much-does-raising-a-child-cost.htm**>.

To Give, or Not to Give?

The reasons for having children are many and varied, but having kids simply because you have enough money to give them the very best of everything is not the usual response. We have children because we can't imagine not having them, because we got pregnant by accident, because we want large families, because we want to be part of something bigger than ourselves. It's not because we think, "Gee, I simply have too much money, I should procreate so I have something to spend it on."

When your precious baby was finally here, did you stay awake at night gazing at their perfect face, promising to give him every new gaming system the minute it hits store shelves? Not likely.

We all want to provide the bare necessities (shelter, nutritious food, medical care, etc.), for our children, but what else is important to you? I created my list knowing that though I'm raising children, I'm developing adults. The qualities I respect in adults are the ones I want to ensure our children have, so they become respected, happy, and productive adults.

I want my children to have safe, comfortable shelter. That doesn't mean we have to live in a 3,500 square foot house, or a house equal in size and grandeur to the other kids my children will befriend. When I was growing up, our home drew the neighbourhood kids in not because of the size of the house or my toy collection, but because my mom was friendly and involved. She planned crafts and activities, baked cookies, and welcomed our friends with open arms.

I want my children to enjoy physical activity. It doesn't mean every child will be enrolled in a different amateur sport for each season, signed up for every skills camp offered, or only own top-of-the-line equipment. It might mean classes at the local recreational centre with loaned gear until they're old enough to appreciate and find value in the more expensive privately run programs. It might only consist of family hikes and walks, pick up street hockey, ice skating at an outdoor rink, or playing catch in the neighbourhood park.

Take a moment with your parenting partner to brainstorm the kinds of things you want to give your children, using the space below to record your ideas.

_____

_____

_____

_____

_____

_____

_____

_____

How well are you meeting these goals? Despite the best intentions, many parents struggling to find enough cash to invest in a Registered Educational Savings Plan (RESP) can look around their homes to discover that the things they have invested their cash in aren't even slightly related to the goals and dreams they have for their children.

You've seen what I want to give my children. Now what don't I want to give them?

- The idea that money equals value, or worth.
- Greed.
- A sense of "being owed something", or entitlement.
- The idea that reward comes without effort.

Let's talk about deprivation. Will my children feel deprived because they don't have the latest video game? Maybe when they're eight. But soon enough they'll realize (with help from mom and dad) that material wealth might come at the expense of personal attention. Sure, Michael down the street may have more expensive toys than our kids do, but are his parents able to attend all of his school plays, volunteer for the school day trip, and not ever open a briefcase or laptop in the evening? Maybe. But the more likely scenario is that Michael's parents can afford to buy him everything he demands because they work long hours, or even more likely, because they've gone deep into debt to do so.

Despite what advertising companies want us to believe, I think that deep down most of us realize that you can't tell a thing about someone's financial situation by looking at what they have and do. A Lexus might be leased and the payments perpetually three months behind. The Montessori preschool fees might be paid by an indulgent grandparent. Many families that take lavish vacations, buy everything new, are constantly redecorating, are actually losing sleep every night on those 800 thread count sheets, hoping they don't drop any balls in their financial juggle. I've listened as very candid friends admitted they couldn't really afford the getaway they were planning, but they just "had to take a vacation—we're so stressed right now." The reason for their stress? Money! Sure, the mini-vacation they had planned wasn't going to be the straw that broke the camel's back, but if they could get their heads around taking control of their finances and not letting their finances control them, they wouldn't need vacations that would ultimately compound their stress. Besides, are vacations really stress relievers? There's often so much to do before you leave, and such a pile of work waiting for you when you get home, it's like you never left at all.

Your children will not be deprived because they wear hand-me-downs and consignment shop finds. But they'd be deprived if you replace your love and attention with video games, lavish birthday parties, and extravagant holidays.

That's not to say all parents who are giving their kids many material things are necessarily depriving them of attention. However, in many cases, that is the trade-off.

I've heard plenty of reasons for why the material items are so important, when savings and paying down debt isn't. One new mom I met insisted used baby equipment was never safe, that used clothing wasn't soft enough for her baby, and substitutions (i.e. using the floor, a bed, or a dresser top in lieu of a change table) were only for parents not truly committed to good parenting. Ouch! Those are easy opinions to hold if you're extremely wealthy, but the rest of us don't have the luxury of having such exacting standards. Unfortunately, many new parents without such deep pockets try to live up to those same standards, either because they feel they have to, or because they don't realize there are other options.

For many parents, it's their nature to make everything look easy, like they have it all together, even when they don't. New parents are the worst culprits. Many people dismiss how difficult being a new parent can be. "It's a breeze," they smile, neglecting to mention they were up for six hours with a screaming baby the previous night. Then when you're up in the middle of the night with your squalling child, you feel as though you're completely alone. *Are we doing something wrong? Why is our baby the only one who can't sleep through the night at three months?* Little do you know, everyone else went through the same thing. They just didn't want you to think they couldn't handle it. I did it too. Pregnant friends came over for dinner and marveled at how clean the house was, how wonderful dinner was, how organized I seemed to be. I now fess up—my mom took the kids for eight hours while I ran my butt off to get the place presentable. A little more honesty in parenting and finances between friends would make both issues far less divisive.

Already have kids? Feel free to skip to the next chapter—the rest of this chapter talks specifically to those who haven't yet decided when they will be having children.

Can We Afford It? An Argument for Waiting

Is there a "right" time to have children? In each family, there are many factors involved in deciding when you're ready to have children. It's not a simple decision. Despite your insistence that it won't (and most couples initially think this), having children will change your lives irrevocably—forever!

As most parents will attest, children are wonderful, and worth the sleep deprivation, arguments, and overextended line of credit. While that is true, it doesn't mean you should decide to have a baby simply because your friend has a newborn that smells like heaven. Children are also a source of stress in your relationship with your husband, friends, career, and finances. Last minute trips to a weekend getaway? Now a rare occurrence. Being available for overtime without notice whenever needed? Impossible—the daycare closes at six. Finding ten minutes to yourself to have a shower? Maybe some days. Quiet dinner with childless friends? Not unless you've paid big bucks for a sitter and gone to the friend's house.

Many very positive parenting skills, such as patience, wisdom, maturity, and confidence in your own ability to make the right choices for your family, come with age. Older mothers may feel less resentful of giving up their wild days—they fully experienced and enjoyed that stage in their life, and are ready for the next adventure, not regretting cutting those days short. Older mothers may feel they've succeeded in their careers and are excited about the next challenge rather than "putting their career on hold" or "sacrificing their career" for a family.

> We kept waiting for the time to be right, because we knew that eventually we wanted to have a family. What we realized was that there isn't really a *right* time to have a baby. I guess we felt that we were as close to *right* as we would ever be. It's a huge commitment ... it changes your life, your perspective—everything. It's expensive. It's exhausting. It's forever. But it's awesome!
>
> *Jen, mom of three*

Because both my children were breastfed and born less than 18 months apart, I really became the parent who stayed home in the evenings to put first one, then two kids to bed. My husband went out two nights a week and I went out only a couple of evenings a year. I had an active social life before kids so there were times staying home every evening was hard on me. The funny thing is that looking back, I can't remember a single event I *missed out on*. Instead, I remember that two-and-a-half-year period with fondness, and treasure my memories of rocking, nursing and singing my babies to sleep.

Nicole, mom of two

Can We Afford Not To? An Argument for Getting Busy Now

With age comes wisdom, and with wisdom, patience. But age can also bring along cynicism, poor health, and decreased energy. One consideration for having children at a younger age is your health. The likelihood of fertility problems increases with age, as does the likelihood of complications in pregnancy. Unfortunately, it's not something that can be predicted. There's no way to tell if waiting will impact your specific chances of a healthy pregnancy. In her book, *Creating a Life: Professional Women and the Quest for Children*, Sylvia Ann Hewlett published the results of a survey she conducted that found that nearly 9 out of 10 young women were confident of their ability to get pregnant in their forties. Yet the American Society for Reproductive Medicine notes that a healthy 30-year-old woman has about a 20% chance per month to get pregnant. By age 40 that chance is only about 5% per month. In many cases, these percentages are true for natural conception as well as conception using advanced reproductive technology.

Yet while you may be at your youthful prime at 22, that isn't necessarily the best time to have children. University of Texas professor John Mirowsky says the best time for women to start bearing children is between ages 27 and 34. Women who wait actually enjoy better health, live longer and end up having healthier babies, Mirowsky argues in a paper he presented at the 2004 American Sociological Association in San Francisco. According to Mirowsky, older mothers tend to be more mature and engage in less risky behaviour, and they are more settled educationally, financially and emotionally.

Remember how your parents would ask, "If your friends jumped off a bridge, would you follow?" Well, my husband and I did. One of our biggest reasons for getting pregnant when we did was because our friends were doing it. Though these friends often complained of getting up six times a night, never having time to themselves, and being perpetually broke, they did seem genuinely happy. We had originally planned on waiting a few more years, but as we began to see our friends less and less, we realized we wanted our children to all grow up together, which would be difficult if our kids were five or six years younger than theirs.

Once we had our first child, we realized why it's easier to hang out with people whose children are the same age as yours. Not only will it lighten your load when you visit (they'll have the same items), but they understand if you fall asleep over dessert at 8:00 pm. Their houses are already childproofed and they understand last minute cancellations because of projectile vomiting (and don't suggest you find a sitter like non-parent friends have done!). Friends without kids are often not as understanding of your busy schedule, they might be quick to be annoyed at normal toddler behaviour, or worse, they might begin offering parental advice that they think is very helpful, which makes you want to slap them.

We also liked the idea of our own parents being young enough to really enjoy their grandchildren. Our parents were hitting their stride when it came to their careers, and had the energy and desire to spend many hours chasing after little ones.

Remember, for every argument for or against having children sooner rather than later, you can find the exception to the rule. You'll find the 45-year-old woman who got pregnant the very first month she tried, the 38-year-old mother who eventually lived to see her grandchildren graduate from university, and the 22-year-old mom who had a child with health problems more common in the babies of older women. Too young, too old? Ultimately, the best time to have children is when you're ready to have children emotionally, physically and financially, according to your own standards.

The Kitchen Table Conversation

It takes two to make a baby, and those two individuals are not always on the same page about when to welcome a little one into the world. I know Keith and I weren't. When I first mentioned that I was ready to get pregnant, he was in shock. For years, we thought we'd be child-free. Once my biological clock starting ticking, I agreed that we should wait until we were in our early thirties. I soon changed my mind. He still wanted to wait, but for the reasons mentioned above, I was convinced it was the right time.

We spent the summer going back and forth over the issue, and eventually he came around to my way of thinking. I ensured he spent lots of time with his buddies who were in the euphoric throes of having new babies—all they did was rave about their kids, and Keith must not have noticed the dark circles under their eyes.

If you're in the same situation, you have a few options. You can hammer the idea into your spouse's head repeatedly. If your partner has a stubborn streak, this is likely a surefire way to ensure they cement their "no kids" position even more firmly into their heads.

Instead of nagging your spouse constantly, agree to set aside time when you can discuss the issue freely, for a limited period of time. Both of you should speak from your own positions, and address the concerns the other person has. Be honest with each other, and remember that if you come to a decision that the other person really isn't happy with, there can be resentment after it's too late to do anything about it.

> After our second son was born, I let my husband know that I hoped to have another child one day. He told me that he was very happy with two and that he wanted to stay that way. I didn't pressure him to have a third, but he eventually came to me to ask when we'd start trying for number three.
>
> *Amber, mom of four*

Final Thought

I clearly remember one point eight months into my first pregnancy, standing at the kitchen island at 2:00 am, popping antacids like they were candy between bouts of sobbing. I was terrified that I had made a huge mistake. We weren't ready. Keith was going to change his mind and hold me responsible for having talked him into it. We were going to be broke, and we'd resent the baby for everything we could no longer afford to do.

As you might guess, my fears were totally unfounded. The moment I held Kate in my arms, I was mesmerized. Keith was too—within moments of the delivery he was asking me, "Aren't you glad we decided to have Kate?" It's something we would say over and over again as the days sped by.

Our timing was right because it was right for us. Whatever your decision, make sure you and your partner are both in agreement, and be sure to present a united front to those rude enough to inquire.

CHAPTER TWO

She's Glowing!

The Price of Pregnancy

WHETHER YOU FOUND YOURSELF PREGNANT by accident, intentionally, or with the help of a medical team, break out the sparkling apple juice—and your calculator. Before you've even bought your first sleeper set, you'll find plenty of pregnancy-related things you need, want, or just can't live without. You've got nine (ten, really) months of challenges to face—including finding a pregnancy wardrobe and deciding what prenatal classes to take—and that's not even covering getting ready for baby's needs (that's all the way in Chapter Seven).

Not Your Mother's Maternity Clothes

Though the next few pages specifically relate to finding maternity clothes, a women's concern, men reading this book may want to skim through them, just to understand why your partner is raiding your closet!

With the exception of a lucky or self-disciplined few, many of us have buried away in our closets a range of clothing that may span five or more dress sizes. Sometimes they're clothes we once fit into, and others are items we picked up on sale that never did fit, but we always hoped someday would. Though the "too tight" items will be of no help to you now, the "too big" items will be wearable for up to the first five months of your pregnancy.

During your pregnancy, you'll likely have to find clothing in different sizes as your belly expands. Most pregnancy pants accommodate this

Money Smart Mom Tip

We started a savings account right away, bought a bag of diapers in different sizes every time we grocery shopped while we still had two incomes, and made sure we really spent time as a couple, because once that baby comes your loving sweetheart is nothing but a dad for a little while.

Melanie, mom of two

through stretchy panels or panels that button, but some items will be comfortable early in the pregnancy and unbearable later. To avoid tight waistbands on your tight budget, it's time to learn how you can save while shopping for maternity clothes.

First Stop: Your Man's Closet

If you've got a man around who wears a larger size than you do, raiding his closet will be your first concession to your new pounds. Men seem to have a larger collection of comfy sweats, track pants and t-shirts, all perfect for bumming around the house and running to the grocery store. You've always loved to cuddle up in his too-large-for-you sweatshirts anyway, and now you have a real excuse.

The First 5 – 10 Pounds

Every pregnant woman hits the stage where she's too big for her regular clothes, but too small for proper maternity clothes. For some, this stage lasts just a few weeks, while for others, it can drag on for a month or two. In your tenth week your breasts may jump two cups sizes. In my first trimester I could no longer button my many fitted shirts. Without a belly though, maternity clothes hung strangely. With no extra cash available to buy shirts that would only fit for a few weeks, I called on all my friends to see if anyone could lend me any larger shirts and sweaters. A few days later I had a brand new collection of tops that fit perfectly. The opposite happened after baby arrived—when I was too small for maternity clothing but couldn't fit into my pre-baby clothing yet, I called on friends to borrow the right sized clothing.

When borrowing clothes from friends, maternity or not, avoid putting them in the uncomfortable position of having to ask you to return the items. When you ask for loaners, assure the lender that you'll be returning each item, as they may have borrowed the clothes from someone else, promised them to someone after you, or plan on being pregnant again themselves. Keep a record of what you received from whom, or ask if you can mark their initials on the tag with a permanent marker. Return each item as soon as you're done with them, and don't forget to enclose a thank-you note.

Money Smart Mom Tip

I was very lucky during my pregnancy and had lots of clothes lent to me. I barely bought anything! Considering you need to create a whole new wardrobe, I think the sharing of clothes is really important, especially between friends. The best idea I've heard of is to start a maternity clothing pool. It gets passed around to various girlfriends and everyone adds a few new pieces to the box as they pass it on. That way you don't have to buy a lot of new clothing; you get an entire wardrobe but still get new pieces that are still in fashion.

Colleen, mom of three

After Your Belly Pops

Up until now you've borrowed clothes from friends, but once your belly has "popped" you'll need proper maternity pants, and maybe a few tops too. Now it's time to call any friends or family members who've had children in the last few years to see if any of them have maternity clothes squirrelled away. Once you've collected as many items as possible from friends and family, you'll have to haul out your wallet and purchase the rest of the things you'll need. Your first stop should be consignment stores. In recent years consignment stores have gained credibility as great places to find quality clothing someone else no longer has a need for.

When buying used maternity wear, be wary of:

- Stained items. Even if it's just lipstick, you may not be able to get the stain out.
- Ill-fitting items. Alterations don't always work, and it's no deal if the item hangs in your closet for your entire pregnancy.
- Versatility. A thick cable-knit sweater might be bargain-priced, but most pregnant women are more comfortable dressing in layers that can be removed, as your hormones wreak havoc with your internal thermostat.

Once you've cleaned out your friends' closets and visited the consignment stores, it's time to fill in the gaps in your wardrobe. Major discount clothing stores now sell reasonably-priced clothing previously only available in expensive specialty shops. Set aside an afternoon to visit a few shops to comparison shop before you buy.

When buying new maternity clothes, there are a few key things to remember:

- Avoid "fake" maternity clothes. True maternity shirts will be longer in the front than the back to accommodate your growing belly without having the back of the shirt hang down to your knees. A fake maternity shirt is simply a large version of a regular shirt. Fake maternity pants won't be made of the same soft material real maternity pants are, a necessity to avoid irritating an often itchy belly.
- Buy the bare minimum. Don't buy 10 shirts and expect to wear them through to the end. Buy five now, and pick up others as the seasons change, your belly expands, and you tire of the other items.
- When selecting pants, choose plain styles. No one will notice you've worn the same three pairs of pants the whole pregnancy if you've selected plain styles. Simple black pants and dark-washed blue jeans are easy staples. Avoid easy-to-remember items with multiple pockets, zippers, or odd colours.

- Stretchy is good, constricting is not. Look for fabrics with a percentage of spandex or elastic.
- Consider investing in a BellaBand®. This seamless knit band is worn at your waistline over your unbuttoned pre-pregnancy pants, over too big maternity pants, or around the waistband of any maternity clothing that falls down, and simply looks like a layered undershirt.
- Choose solids over patterns, dark clothes over light. Black pieces are easy to mix and match, hide stains better, and are less memorable. Use funky and inexpensive accessories to brighten your look.
- If your feet swell, look for inexpensive slip-on shoes with a low heel to get you through to the end.

"It doesn't matter how awful some of the free items you're given are," says Amber, mom of two. "Pregnancy is beautiful. People you don't know will tell you that you look radiant and touch your belly, even if you're wearing a tent!"

Get Outta Town

If you live in a small town, rural area, or even just a city lacking in retail outlets for inexpensive maternity wear, it might be worthwhile to take a short trip to a nearby city with better selection and prices, or even leave the country with a few clicks of the mouse. When my local stores offered nothing but matronly-looking shirts for $45, I went online and discovered an American website offering fashionable shirts for as low as US $10. Even after factoring in the exchange rate, shipping costs, and customs fees, the shirts I ordered were no more than CDN $25, and they carried me through with compliments until after the birth.

The Essentials

For some, the increase in breast size during pregnancy is a thrilling treat, even if shelling out for a few new bras isn't. Though maternity bras are widely available, they aren't cheap, and many moms don't bother buying them. Certain brands of bras from lingerie stores or department stores will be just as comfortable, and many women swear by sports bras to provide the soft comfort and serious support they need.

As for your underoos, again, you'll probably want to skip the maternity section. You can find comfortable underwear in the regular stores that will accommodate your bump. Look for bikini cuts that sit low in the rear (maternity pants are often low riders) and under your belly. If you wore thongs before pregnancy, you may never need to give them up; investing in a few in a larger size might be your only concession.

The Home Stretch

As you get closer to your due date, some of the items that fit perfectly for the past few months may seem uncomfortably tight, and if you left some room in your budget for this home stretch, now's the time to spend it. Also, if your breasts have stayed the same size for the past few months, they're likely to start growing again as they fill with milk. If you're planning on trying to breastfeed, any bras you buy in the last few months should be nursing bras. Don't buy too many at once though; if you end up bottle-feeding you'll fit back into your old bras sooner than you think.

Take the Clothes, and the Advice

There is one thing pregnant ladies get too much of for free—advice. As annoying as it can be, sometimes a little advice is worth heeding. While pregnant I worked in an office with plenty of pregnant ladies and new moms, and when I announced my news, they showered me with shopping tips. I was cautioned against buying any pants that covered my whole belly, as it was supposed to be uncomfortable. Anything with a turtleneck would supposedly be too hot, and anything with a wide or scoop neck would mean I'd constantly be trying to hide the straps of my sturdy new bras. When the fifth mom gave me the same advice, I decided their rules were law, and avoided these items.

I even received shopping advice from complete strangers. Trying on a comfortable cotton shirt on sale for just $25, another mom-to-be, many months farther along than my four months, cautioned me against it. "It's not long enough in the front," she pointed out. "It'll end up above your belly button by the time you hit your seventh month." When I compared it against other, more expensive shirts in the store, it was far shorter than the others. It might have been okay for a month or two, but soon enough it would be too short. I appreciated her advice (though not the fact that her two-year-old was running wild in the store and pulling open the curtains of occupied changing rooms).

Money Smart Mom Tip

If you grow out of some maternity items before the end of your pregnancy, don't be too quick to get rid of them. They might be just right for the weeks and months after baby's born, before you fit back into your regular clothing.

Advice passed on from another mom shopping at a maternity store.

Product Overload

One expense sometimes underestimated is how much you'll spend on a number of little things. Prenatal vitamins, a cocoa butter stretch mark prevention stick, a body pillow, anti-nausea medication—the little things can add up quickly.

As with any other purchase, many things are simply not a necessity. If something is a true need, find ways to spend as little as possible on the item. Generic products are often as good as name brand ones, or better. For instance, most studies claim that stretch mark creams and lotions do nothing to prevent the marks, which are more the result of your genetics, but they can provide comfort for an itchy belly. You don't need to buy an overpriced pregnancy stick—any moisturizing lotion will do, including a generic brand from your local drugstore.

Nesting

During the latter half of your pregnancy, you may find yourself being asked, "Are you nesting yet?" The nesting urge strikes females of nearly all mammals, and it may manifest itself in an uncontrollable desire to clean the house, finish old projects, and even tie up emotional loose ends! I've even heard of a woman who leaped out of bed at 3:00 am, woke up her husband and forced him to pull out the fridge and stove, just so she could scrub behind them. Hopefully, your nesting instinct won't push you quite that far! But you can use the nesting urge to your advantage both emotionally and financially.

If you have the urgent desire to keep yourself busy, borrow a few cookbooks from the library and spend a weekend creating meals to freeze for after baby's arrival, when one of the things you'll feel least like doing is cooking. This will fulfill the nesting instinct, and save you from deciding to order pricey takeout. During this time, you'll be amazed to find you consider decluttering your home to be soothing, and if you hold a garage sale with all the stuff you've culled, you'll also make a few bucks.

Decisions, Decisions

Though I'll go into the stay-at-home vs. working parent debate in Chapter Three, pregnancy is the time to be thinking about any lifestyle changes you want to make before children come along, or changes you'll want to make soon after. Will you need a house with a third bedroom or can your kids bunk together for a few years? Is it time to trade the dirt bike in for a little red wagon? Keep in mind that while it's important to discuss potential changes, it's advisable not to make rash decisions that have come from out of left field. The experience of having a newborn is stressful enough without adding additional stressors such as a big move. Also, once baby is here, you may find things you once considered important to be irrelevant. However, some moms feel differently.

Prenatal Education

If you don't know the first thing about babies, or want to ensure what you do know is correct and up-to-date, prenatal classes are for you. Prenatal classes are designed to provide you with helpful information about your pregnancy, labour and delivery, and parenthood. Classes are taught by trained professionals, and most cover the basics: good health during pregnancy, what to expect during labour and delivery, preparing yourself and your home for the newborn, what to expect at the hospital, breastfeeding, etc. Some classes include a hospital tour, while others teach you how to install your car seat. Read the class brochure to decide which classes you're interested in. While some basic classes are free, others may have a small fee involved. If you're a low-income family, you may be eligible to receive a fee reimbursement—check with the registration office.

Another Ultrasound Please ...

If you have a low-risk, routine pregnancy, you'll likely be booked for just one or two ultrasounds. These medically-required ultrasounds are to meet the doctor's needs—not yours. If you're looking for a loving, bonding experience, or even to simply find out the gender of your baby, there are no guarantees you'll get either.

That's why many parents turn to "entertainment" ultrasounds offered by private companies in many large cities. These ultrasound appointments are touted as a bonding-oriented experience using traditional 2-D or the more advanced 3-D technology. Friends and family are welcome to attend, and the scan is displayed on a large television monitor and recorded. The price ranges from $120 to $200, depending on the type of scan.

There are opponents and proponents of the business. The case against having an entertainment ultrasound is based on the potential risk of all ultrasounds. An ultrasound employs high frequency sound waves which bounce back to create an image of bodily structures. In prenatal care, they're performed to determine the size, location or age of the developing fetus, the number of developing fetuses, and to check for birth defects, fetal movement and heartbeat. Ultrasounds are routine; their use has been considered safe for more than thirty years, and most pregnant women in Canada have one or more over the course of their pregnancy. Though there have been studies that suggest repeated ultrasound exposure increases the likelihood of left-handedness, a possible result of subtle brain damage, the results of these studies are widely debated. More recent research proposes a link between ultrasounds and autism.

Proponents of entertainment ultrasounds defend the practice, arguing that commercial ultrasounds can improve the bond between mother and baby, resulting in improved prenatal care. They also note that many doctors regularly refer their patients to their service, and that in some European countries, doctors offer ultrasounds at every visit. If you can afford it, it's ultimately your decision.

Final Thought

As you can see, adding a child to your family can be anything but simple. Whether the child is conceived easily, through the help of medical technology or given from one family to another in the case of adoption, the child will be equally loved. Speaking of love—who is going to be responsible for undertaking the day to day raising of your precious loved one? Does love have anything to do with it, or is it all about the money? Chapter Three offers an analysis of both sides of the debate.

The Basics

I N A PERFECT WORLD, YOU'D have got your hands on this book before you got pregnant. However, you might be reading it after already having one, two, or more kids. So this is a back-to-basics chapter. It's going to address concepts that are important to grasp regardless of your situation now.

Are you both working parents, or is mom or dad at home? Are you happy with the situation or are you reading this book hoping it can help you make changes?

Wading into the working parents vs. stay-at-home parents debate is not for the faint of heart. The decision for one parent to stay at home, or for both to work, is not one made easily, and it's an issue fraught with emotion—mainly guilt! While one mom may vehemently defend her desire to go back to work just months after birth, she may actually feel guilty for not wanting or not being able to stay at home. A stay-at-home dad may feel as though he made the wrong decision, and wish to return to the structure of an office. Career-driven moms may look down their noses at the yoga pant wearing stay-at-home moms, while the stay-at-home mom believes the working-outside-the-home mom isn't being a responsible parent, and that if they just tried harder, one parent could afford to stay home.

Study after study proves that children with a parent at home are happier, healthy, smarter, and better adjusted. And study after study proves exactly the opposite!

A majority of Canadians (71%) either "strongly" (43%) or "somewhat" (28%) agree that, "a parent who does not work and stays home to raise the children," provides the best child care, and 76% of working parents with children in child care would prefer to have a parent stay home.

There's also the notion that sending your kids to daycare means you're letting a stranger raise your kids. But what about sending them to school? Why does having a mom at home count so much when the child is two, but when the child is five, mom's "allowed" to go back to work and let teachers take over? Now that my first daughter is four and I'm spending more time with her during the day than I did when she was one and in full-time care, I'm glad I did it this way! Sure, she was adorable as a baby, but she's a riot as a preschooler. She's way more fun to be around now, as we can have real conversations, and do things like fun craft projects and baking together. My time with her now seems to be making a bigger impact on her personality than the time I spent with her when she was just five-months-old.

> Children cared for by adults other than just mom or dad also may find the different caregiving styles beneficial. I firmly believe that our children learn from others. Often parents have one style for parenting and teaching their children, and someone else may have fresh ideas or a different approach that may reach that child more effectively.
>
> *Angela, mom of two*

Running the Numbers

You don't have to decide whether you'll be a stay-at-home parent or working parent the moment you conceive. In fact, many moms enthusiastically plan on going back to work after their maternity leave is up, only to discover themselves dreading their return to the workforce. There's more information available in Chapter Nine about work and child care options once your maternity or parental leave is up.

I've heard many childless couples, or couples where the earning potential of one parent is far less than the other, assert that, "If you just cut back on expenses, one parent can stay home with the kids." There's the idea that the second income is eaten up completely by taxes, daycare, and work-related expenses. If this were always true, I suspect you'd see

Children Enrolled in Day Care Get a Head Start in School

Results from analyses of data from the latest release of the National Longitudinal Survey of Children and Youth suggest that children who are enrolled in early childhood programs and daycare centres appear to get a head start in school over youngsters who stay at home with a parent.

The analysis compared the level of performance of two groups of children in kindergarten. The first group included those who, during the 1994–95 school year, attended an early childhood program, a daycare centre, or received care from a paid worker such as a nanny, a non-relative or a relative other than the mother or the father of the child. The second group of children were those who stayed at home with a parent, who in 90% of the cases was their mother. Two years later, the children in the first group were faring better at school.

About 40% of children who were in an early childhood program at ages three and four were judged by their teachers as being near the top of their kindergarten class in communication skills, as opposed to only 25% who did not participate in such programs. Also, 38% of these children were rated by their teachers as being near the top of their kindergarten class in learning skills, compared with 24% of kindergarten children who did not attend an early childhood program.

The study also found that higher proportions of children who attended early childhood programs were able to write a simple sentence, compare numbers and understand simple concepts of time, such as *today*, *summer*, and *bedtime*. These relationships held true regardless of the education of the child's mother or the income of the household.

a lot more one-income households. Yes, your spending habits do have a lot to do with your work situation, but sometimes it's not so easy to decide the right path. I've met moms working for what amounts to less than $200 a month after child care and working costs, but that $200 is the difference between buying their own groceries and relying on the food bank. I've met other moms who gave up an income of $70,000 a year to stay at home with just one child. If you only consider the financial implications of such a decision, it may not result in the most practical outcome. However, emotionally it was the right one for them, and they have been able to make their household budget work.

Nicole had always intended to go back to work after one year. She planned on working full-time for six months after her first child in order to have her children 18 months apart and still be eligible to receive full benefits and a second year of maternity leave. However, after she met her first baby, her plans changed. "I fell in love with her the moment she was born, but she was a very difficult baby. Even her grandparents would call us home when we left them to babysit during the first year!"

Nicole was already pregnant again when she and her husband realized there was no way they could leave their daughter in the care of someone who didn't already love her.

> We regrouped, crunched the numbers, and I ended up staying home for two and a half years after she was born and one year after my son was born. The 18 months I didn't earn any income were financially difficult, but much better for our family and especially our daughter. We even had to sell a car to live off the proceeds for a few months. But it all worked out and we've never regretted our decision to keep me at home for those years. Now I work part-time, and love the balance I have between work and being with my wonderful kids.
>
> *Nicole, mother of two*

One couple I know has a great arrangement. They're in their thirties and have two children under four. Mom works from home in the mornings while dad handles the kids, then dad heads into the office in the afternoon while mom is home, and her full attention is on the kids. They outsource everything—their recycling pick-up, house cleaning, even grocery shopping sometimes. They are dedicated to spending a lot of time with their children, and being in the moment with their kids. What's the catch? They're both engineers and well respected in their profession. Though both their salaries are reduced because they work less than their colleagues, their combined income is still far more than it would be if only one of them were working full-time. If a warehouse forklift driver and his sales clerk wife wanted this arrangement, there is no way they'd

She Said What?

During a speech in Toronto, Alberta's Finance Minister, Iris Evans, landed in hot water over her statements on the issue of working vs. stay-at-home parents. In talking about her own children, she said, "They've understood perfectly well that when you're raising children, you don't both go off to work and leave them for somebody else to raise. This is not a statement against daycare. It's a statement about their belief in the importance of raising children properly." Evans later clarified her statements, telling the *Calgary Herald* that she didn't intend to suggest two-income parents weren't caring for their children properly. "If it came across as if I was undervaluing them as parents, that's totally wrong and I would apologize for that. I certainly didn't intend that." She was lambasted in the press and from constituents outraged that Evans seemed to be condemning families in which both parents worked.

Her initial statement and subsequent backpedaling made me cringe. Luckily, she's not my mother-in-law. Her gaffe is a lesson for all of us. While you may believe a strongly about who should take care of the children and when, speaking out strongly on the topic could upset others around you who are not of the same mind.

have the money available for outsourcing anything, never mind the occasional special event dinner out. Their part-time salaries may not cover their housing.

There are many risks to leaving the workforce. Even if you manage to cover your day-to-day expenses, are you able to keep contributing to your investments? Will you lose out on extra contributions you would have made to your mortgage? What about your career? In the years you'll be at home would you have received a raise or a promotion? Will your future earning potential be hindered by your years at home?

Do the Math

To know if you can make it work on one income, you'll need to know how you're making things work now. This involves facing reality. Many people are afraid to balance their chequebook, open their credit card statement, or talk with their creditors. It may seem easier just to try and ignore the problem, ignore the phone calls from collection agencies, and ignore your increasing credit card balance. It's not though—and increasing rates of bankruptcy in Canada prove ignorance is not bliss. Eventually, you will have to get real about your finances. You might not face them until you're trying to get approved for a bigger mortgage, a nicer car, or until one of you loses your job or your hours are cut back at work. Worse, you might not face them until the bank sends someone to the door to repossess your car. But the day of reckoning will come; why not make it today? By starting today, and retaking control of your finances, you will end up feeling better about your finances moving forward. Furthermore, you'll be creating the opportunity to reverse spending trends and start a saving habit before you're too far in debt to ever dig out without declaring bankruptcy.

Where does your family stand financially? How is your credit is being affected? What can you do to turn things around? You can't know where you're going if you don't know where you've been. Pick up a pencil and fill out the form on the opposite page to calculate your net worth.

The net worth statement is a summary of your financial position at a particular point in time. It is a list of all your financial assets and all of your financial liabilities. Net worth is the dollar amount you have when you subtract everything you owe from everything you own.

Your net worth is a snapshot of your financial health. It's helpful to create a net worth statement annually, to ensure your worth is increasing instead of following a downward trend.

If you're quite young, you will likely have negative net worth. There are no set rules about how much your net worth should be based on your age, income and number of children, but there are averages.

Statistics Canada has released a report based on their Survey of Financial Security, undertaken in 2005. The median net worth by the age of main breadwinner of the household is as follows (see p. 28):

Calculating Your Net Worth

ASSETS:
- House $ _____
- Other Real Estate $ _____
- Vehicles $ _____
- Other Significant Material Assets $ _____
- Bank Accounts $ _____
- Non-registered Investments $ _____
- Registered Investments $ _____
- RESPs $ _____
- Other $ _____
- Other $ _____
- Other $ _____

- **Total Assets** (A) $ _____

LIABILITIES:
- Mortgage $ _____
- Car Loans $ _____
- Student Loans $ _____
- Credit Cards $ _____
- Line of Credit $ _____
- Other $ _____
- Other $ _____
- Other $ _____

- **Total Liabilities** (L) $ _____

- **Net Worth** (W) [A – L = W] $ _____

NB: Total Assets (A) – Total Liabilities (L) = Net Worth (W).

- Under 35 – $15,000
- 35 to 44 – $140,000
- 45 to 54 – $230,000
- 55 to 64 – $407,000
- 65 and older – $300,000

How do you measure up to the rest of the country? More importantly, how do you feel about where you are today?

Budgeting—Eeek!

Now that you know where you stand financially, do you know how you got there? What are you doing right, and what are you doing wrong?

Comparing your family financials to a small business is an easy analogy. To ensure your business is successful you can't bounce cheques or run out of cash before your invoices are paid. You also need to be able to invest in your business.

If you want your family unit to run smoothly, you also can't bounce cheques, run out of cash before payday, and you should be investing in your family's future.

While most businesses track their spending to ensure they're putting their money towards items that provide the highest value for their dollar, most families don't track their spending at all. If there's money in the account they buy what they need or want, and if there's any left at the end of the month, it can be put towards savings. Unfortunately, with this type of financial management there's rarely anything left over at the end of the month.

Are you certain that all of your money is being spent on necessities? How can you be sure if you don't have a record of where your money is going?

If you can't say with certainty and accuracy how much you spend on things each month, how can you be sure you're making wise financial decisions? On the Canadian reality television show, *Till Debt Do Us Part*, host and financial expert Gail Vaz-Oxlade has couples write out a list of what they think they spend each month. Then Gail shows them what they're actually spending. The numbers are always astonishing. Sometimes the couples are spending four to five times what they think they're spending in many areas, especially when it comes to finance or interest charges on their debt. They also always significantly underestimate their level of consumer (non-mortgage) debt and their rampant consumerism. Are you aware of exactly how much you actually spend on home decor each month? Groceries? Debt interest? Bank service fees?

Completing the worksheet found on pages 30–31 will take a bit of research on your part. First, gather your bank statements and credit card statements and fill in as many columns as you can based on your past spending. Some numbers may be guesses, especially if you often take out large amounts of cash and buy items such as gas and groceries without keeping receipts or recording the cash purchases.

Next, track your spending for one month, by collecting receipts into a folder (mark on ATM slips what you spent the cash on), or by updating the totals as you spend.

Now that you more fully understand your financial situation, you can decide what your next steps should be. It's unlikely that you've looked at the worksheet and said to your spouse, "Look honey, your income isn't being spent on anything at all! Of course you can stay home with the kids!" Hopefully, if your goal is for one parent to work fewer hours or not work at all, you've found areas that, with the help of the rest of this book, you can trim your expenditures to the bare essentials.

Creating a System

It's simply not enough to know what you spent last month on everything, and assume that now that you realize you spend way too much money on eating out, that you'll magically spend less doing so and suddenly have an extra $200 in the bank each month. If you're serious about getting your family finances in order, you'll have to track your spending for a long, long time. Maybe forever. If you don't, it's unlikely you'll stay on track, and you'll slip into old habits quickly. Just as most people who have successfully lost a lot weight and kept it off maintain a food journal, financial savers save more money when they keep a spending journal.

Calculating Your Net Disposable Monthy Income

INCOME (before taxes):	Estimated	Actual
• Dad's Main Income	$	$
• Dad's Secondary Income	$	$
• Mom's Main Income	$	$
• Mom's Secondary Income	$	$
• Other Sources of Income	$	$
• **Total Income:**	$	$

EXPENSES:	Estimated	Actual
• Dad's Income Tax	$	$
• Dad's Payroll Deductions	$	$
• Mom's Income Tax	$	$
• Mom's Payroll Deductions	$	$
• RRSPs/Investments	$	$
• RESPs	$	$
• Life Insurance	$	$
• Rent/Mortgage	$	$
• Property Tax	$	$
• Home Insurance	$	$
• Home Alarm	$	$
• Utilities:		
– Hydro	$	$
– Natural Gas	$	$
– Water	$	$
– Sewer	$	$
• Telephone:		
– Landline	$	$
– Cellular	$	$
• Cable TV	$	$
• Internet	$	$
• Groceries	$	$

Calculating Your Net Disposable Monthy Income – cont.

EXPENSES – continued: Estimated   Actual

	Estimated	Actual
• Miscellaneous Household	$	$
• Child care	$	$
• School Fees	$	$
• Medical	$	$
• Dental	$	$
• Car Insurance	$	$
• Car Loan/Lease Payment	$	$
• Automobile Gas	$	$
• Car Repairs	$	$
• Parking	$	$
• Transit	$	$
• Line of Credit Payment	$	$
• Credit Card Payments	$	$
• Student Loan Payment	$	$
• Dad's Clothing	$	$
• Mom's Clothing	$	$
• Kids' Clothing	$	$
• Miscellaneous Personal	$	$
• Memberships	$	$
• Subscriptions	$	$
• Entertainment	$	$
• Gifts	$	$
• Pets	$	$
• Vacation	$	$
• Charitable Donations	$	$
• **Total Expenses:**	$	$

There are a number of different methods you can use to set up a program for tracking your household spending and savings. It's important to have this discussion with your partner, as you'll need their buy in for this to work. If you use an envelope system and put $150 into the lunch money envelope but find $300 worth of debit withdrawals at fast food restaurants, it's going to lead to battles.

Count on Your Computer

If you're into computers, one simple way to track your spending is to set up a spreadsheet, or purchase a budgeting software program. There are fantastic spreadsheets available for free downloading at <**www.office. microsoft.com**>. I use a program (Budget Ace) that I purchased over the Internet for $24 at <**www.download.com**>. It allows me to enter our income, track daily spending by category, create graphs and charts, and see how much we exceeded or saved in each category.

Every evening I take a moment to use my online bank statement to enter any electronic transactions, and my agenda to transfer the notes I made whenever I spent cash. When I make purchases at department or discount stores, I keep the receipts to break down the total amount spent into the right categories. Paper towels and toilet paper go into Miscellaneous Household, not Groceries, even if I bought them at the grocery store.

Easy Envelopes

With the envelope (or jars) system, you set up a series of envelopes each month or week marked with the category the money can be spent on. On payday, leave enough money in the bank to cover automatic withdrawals such as your mortgage or rent, and your savings. The rest of the money gets divided up according to how much you want to spend on each category each month or week. When an envelope is empty, don't spend anything else on that category for the remainder of the time period—and no stealing from other envelopes. Any money left over in an envelope at the end of the week or month should be added to your debt repayment or savings, or tucked into a special envelope, such as a Christmas gifts or vehicle repair envelope.

Motivation Through Money Clubs

A money club is not the same thing as an investment club. Investment club members pool financial contributions and investment advice to invest in companies or stocks in order to gain from each other's wisdom and buying power. A money club is a group of people who get together to have frank discussions about their finances, keeping each other accountable and providing positive support when it comes to staying on the right financial track. The Canadian gurus of money clubs are Andrea Baxter, Angela Self, Katie Dunsworth, Robyn Gunn and Sandra Hanna, the co-authors of *Smart Cookies Guide to Making More Dough and Getting Out of Debt*. If you think the outside accountability factor would be helpful to you, the Smart Cookies girls can help. The book is an inspiring read, and will give you the tools to set up your own money club.

Personal Help

Personal financial coaches are available in most major Canadian cities. These coaches may offer some services similar to a debt management service in that they may offer consolidation financing. However, many are simply personal coaches working on a per hour fee basis. These folks are experts in budgeting, spending, and saving. Much like hiring a fitness trainer can help you get your workouts started and organized or take them to the next level, a good money coach can help you understand where you are financially if you're finding the task overwhelming. They can also help you make fine-tuning decisions when it comes to your spending and saving. Sometimes reading books about money (like this one!) isn't enough to get you motivated to take control—it might take one-on-one counselling to get you on track. If you have a financial advisor, they may offer this type of service as well.

When looking for a financial coach, be sure to check their references and follow up with the Better Business Bureau and your local Chamber of Commerce for a history of their business practices.

Part of having a household budget is having a budget for the future too. Do you know how much money you'll have in your RRSPs in six years? How much debt will you be in nine years from now? Your current household budget will show you where you can make changes to repay

Your Credit Report

Your credit history is maintained by credit bureaus. These private companies collect information reported to them by banks and other creditors. Credit bureaus are permitted to report accurate negative credit information for seven years, and bankruptcy information for 6 to 14 years. This negative credit information cannot be deleted from your record within this time frame. Only information that is inaccurate can be corrected.

You can request a free copy of your credit report from Equifax Canada Inc <www.equifax.ca> or Trans Union of Canada <www.transunion.ca>. Once you've received it, check it over to ensure it is accurate. You can deal with any mistakes yourself at no charge, and contact information for corrections is included in the report.

If you have bad credit, the only way to fix it is time, and by improving your financial profile. You might have seen ads promoting companies that will clear up your credit report or fix your credit. These are credit score repair scams—the companies are not reputable, and can't do what they promise. After you pay ridiculously high fees, they usually disappear with your money. Other companies will take your money, then provide you with a report showing that the bad credit has been removed. They do this by submitting multiple requests to the credit bureau to verify the information. If the credit bureau cannot verify an entry within 60 days, it will remove the information from the report. However, when the information is later verified to be accurate, it will go back in the report.

You should get a copy of both your own credit report and your spouse's every year. Like Ronald Reagan used to say, *Trust, but Verify*. Many people, female and male alike, have been burned because they had no idea their spouse had mounting credit card debt on secret cards.

debt or increase savings, and a cash flow statement will help you make a realistic plan for the future. What job changes might you want to make in a few years? What travel plans are important to you? By creating a cash flow plan you can work out where you need to start saving for certain life events, and it gives you a benchmark against which you can check your progress.

What to Do with Debt

The sooner you get rid of your debt, the better. This book will give you a lot of tools to live more frugally and save more money, and this can be used to pay down any debt you may have. But if you are struggling with how much to pay back, understanding good debt versus bad debt, or just don't know how to handle your debt load, again, a resource book I highly recommend *Debt-Free Forever* by Gail Vaz-Oxlade.

Some parents believe debt is a necessary part of life—perhaps beginning with student loans, they've never lived without debt payments. A lot of people just don't make their debt a priority. They make the minimum payments because they never have any extra to put towards it, yet somehow find the cash for brand new craft supplies, stylish new clothing for their kids, a few vacations a year, and concert tickets. They live a lifestyle their income can't support without debt, and usually it's debt that is slowly creeping higher and higher. The worst part is that they're often not saving anything for the future either, because if they won't trim their expenses to find the extra cash for debt repayment, it certainly isn't there for savings.

According to the Financial Consumer Agency of Canada's 2008 Youth Financial Literacy Study, almost 56% of Canadians between the ages of 18 and 29 caring for a child report that there has been at least one month in the past year when they did not have enough money to cover their expenses. When this happens, they borrow from family or friends or use credit cards to cover the shortfall.

If you're so deeply into debt that you can't even afford to make the minimum payments, you might be able to avoid bankruptcy by meeting with your creditors, attending credit counseling, taking out a debt consolidation loan, or, depending on your province of residency, applying for a Consolidation Order. A Consolidation Order establishes the amount and the times when payments are due to the court. The court will distribute your payments to your creditors over a period of three years, a process which frees you from creditor harassment and wage garnishment. You also do not lose your assets.

You could also try a Consumer Proposal. Under the Bankruptcy and Insolvency Act you may make a proposal to your creditors to reduce the amount of your debts, extend the time you have to pay off the debt, or provide some combination of both. Until your consumer proposal is withdrawn, rejected, or otherwise ended, your creditors cannot attempt to recover their debts outside of the program.

Let's say you owe $10,000 on a credit card, and your minimum monthly payment is $250. Using the consumer proposal, you can propose that you will pay $150 each month until the debt is paid. You could also propose that you will only pay back $7,000 of the debt. While this may seem like an easy way to avoid paying your bills, it's not. Though you'll get some help from the government, there is a mountain of paperwork you'll need to complete, and it isn't free. Also, creditors do not have to accept the proposal. If the proposal is rejected, it's open season again on your assets and wages. And like a bankruptcy, a Consumer Proposal is a black mark on your credit report.

There are a number of companies advertising how they can help you restore your credit or emerge from debt. Most major cities will have both public and private debt counseling services. You may be able to find a not-for-profit service with either a low fee or even no fee at all. You could also speak with a certified independent financial advisor or your bank may offer a credit counseling service. There are a number of private companies now available that provide credit counseling services for large fees, which they often justify because of the money they'll save you over the long run. Be wary of any of these programs if their fees seem too high, or if they come at you with a hard sell. Be sure to get a written quote and take that to someone like your banker for a second opinion. Your banker may be able to handle many of your requests at no charge, or at least explain the benefits and risks of the financial decisions being recommended.

The Last Resort

Bankruptcy is your last resort. Though it sounds ideal—your debts will be erased, and your creditors are not allowed to contact or harass you—it's quite a dire situation to be in. Everything you own, except a few items, will be sold and the money raised will go to your creditors. Your credit report will show your bankruptcy for anything from 6 to 14 years, depending on your province of residency and any previous bankruptcies. With it on your report, you'll have a hard time getting a mortgage, credit card, loan, or even a cell phone. You may even be denied employment. Financial institutions and other companies that require employees be bonded will generally not hire you if you have a bankruptcy on file.

It's important to realize that if you declare bankruptcy but one of your debts was co-signed, your co-signer is now responsible for that debt. Also, student loan debts are not absolved by bankruptcy, nor are child support obligations. Going bankrupt isn't free either—you'll owe $1,000 or more to the bankruptcy trustee—and this isn't absolved by the bankruptcy. So once you're out of debt by bankruptcy, you're right back in it again.

One Budget or Two?

Sharing your life doesn't necessarily mean sharing your bank account. Many couples choose to keep their finances separate. This can breed frustration and resentment if one partner is earning and spending more than the other partner is able to, and they feel left out of the fun. You could split your expenses evenly, or the spouse earning the higher salary could contribute a proportionately higher amount to the household budget.

If you have irreconcilable differences over the handling of your disposable income, splitting your finances may be the best move. If one partner is a spendthrift and prone to spending grocery money on new golf clubs, setting up a rigid system where the more financially responsible partner controls the combined income for bills, debt repayment, and savings may be the best solution. Separate savings programs and daily banking accounts may also make sense if you're in a volatile relationship where you think someday you may want access to savings that your partner can't touch.

If you do have joint finances, or if one partner handles all of the financials, ensure the other person is still creating a credit history by having some bills or a credit card in their own name.

Preparing for a One-Income Household

If you've decided to transition to a one-income family during maternity leave, after going back to work for a short while, or even after your five kids have started school, you'll need to prepare for your new financial situation.

First, you should understand your total household contribution. The individual considering giving up their income would look at what it costs in terms of money not coming into the home, and money that wouldn't need to be spent because the parent would be home. For instance, if dad stays home, he won't need to pay for daycare, business clothing, lunches with colleagues, contributions to office gifts, or even the second family car. There are certain tax breaks for single-income families as well. If both parents work outside the home, income tax law requires that the lower-income earning spouse deducts the child-care expenses. If one parent stays at home, the working spouse can claim a small spousal credit.

What does the working parent who is considering staying home currently spend on the following?

- House cleaning
- Work clothes
- Coffee breaks
- Breakfast and lunches out
- Takeout and fast food dinners for the family
- Child care
- Gas and parking fees
- A second vehicle

After running the numbers, many families find that it just makes sense for one parent to stay at home with the children. In others, the decision is much more difficult. How large is the income gap? With changes in your spending and consumption, is the gap too large, or manageable? Would a part-time weekend or evening job cover the deficit?

Recommended Surfing

At <*www.todaysparent.ca*> choose "Parent
Time" and look under "Tools" for the Stay-at-home
calculator. This quick worksheet will allow you to
enter in your income, child care costs, tax bracket,
and work-related expenses to determine your total
contribution to the household.

Many stay-at-home parents must find a way to contribute some income without resorting to putting their child into pricey child care. Though we usually think of working parents as those working in a traditional 9 to 5 job, a significant proportion of Canadians work non-traditional hours. Compressed work weeks, flexible work arrangements, night shifts, weekends only—there are many different arrangements available depending on your industry and employer.

Parents sometimes switch careers, either temporarily or permanently, to accommodate more time at home. You may be able to telecommute, start a home-based business, or work for someone else's home-based business. The nice woman who drives your child's school bus and brings her one-year-old along for the ride works just four to six hours a day and has her child with her. She gets paid, plus avoids child care costs. And she just may have a university degree and an extensive background in sales. The call centre employee who takes your call at 2:00 am may have once been an executive in the same company who decided to work just enough night shifts to cover his family's income gap.

A word of caution though—if you're working at home you may still require child care, and you may pay the same amount you would have if you had your child in care full time.

If you've figured out that your full-time job is only netting you $500 a month, you could work part-time to make a portion of that amount, and cut your spending to make up the shortfall. The following list of suggestions for alternative work for parents may inspire you to think of other means by which to earn additional income.

- Drive a school bus
- Offer evening and weekend babysitting
- Deliver newspapers
- Operate a home-based child care
- Become a home party sales consultant
- Create a freelancing or in-home business in your area of expertise (tutoring, writing, music lessons, etc.)
- Join a virtual office company in your area
- Work as a casual employee, on occasional weekends or evenings when you have access to free child care (spouse or relatives)
- Work temporary jobs, such as seasonal retail help
- Find an employer that will allow you to bring your child to work (it sounds strange, but they do exist!)

Direct Marketing Home-Based Businesses

There are literally hundreds of work-at-home sales opportunities that rely on direct sales and party or event hosting to sell the product. Food lovers can sell food storage containers, cooking utensils, or spice mixes. If you have a large mom network, you could focus on children's toys, products, or books. If you have an outgoing personality, you could also try selling sex toys or demonstrating pole dancing.

For every mom who makes big bucks selling products like these, there are many, many more who sell to a few friends and family members and no one else. It's easy to host the first few parties when your friends are willing to do you the favour, but far more difficult to convince strangers to host parties and buy the products you're hawking. It takes a very dedicated and passionate person to make these sorts of distributed, multi-level marketing businesses real money-makers. You'll need to get comfortable with sales techniques, hosting sales parties, and lose all inhibitions about making cold calls or approaching strangers.

A close friend of mine began selling a home party product and I felt very guilty about not hosting a party for her. In my opinion the products she was selling were overpriced and unnecessary. When I finally came clean, we talked openly about why she was selling the products. She was hoping to make a little extra cash without having to put her children in child care. After the start-up fee, the cost of her catalogues, and her travel costs driving to customers' houses, she actually made very little profit, and was unwittingly alienating all of her friends. Worse still, when she actually tracked her hours over a period of two weeks and included every minute she spent preparing and hosting parties, making calls, delivering product or being available for customers to pick up products, dropping off catalogues and placing orders, she made much less than the provincial minimum wage per hour.

The truth is, most women don't need the products that home party businesses are selling, can get a reasonable facsimile for far less elsewhere, and feel guilty about pressuring their friends into attending such events. If you're a stay-at-home mom on a budget, do you have $90 to spend on plastic containers when perfectly good substitutes are available for a fraction of the price at the grocery store? Do you have $80 to blow on six cute childrens' books, when the kids already have bookcases full and you can get great books at garage sales and thrift stores for under $1 each?

If you've decided it's still worthwhile, then be sure to pick a product that's a good fit for you, and for which you feel there is a real and growing demand. It may be difficult to get your network of twenty-something friends to agree to host a cosmetics party, but a pole dancing party may have them lining up in droves to book for stagettes and birthdays. Before signing up with a company, ask your friends and family if they've heard of the company, what they think of their products and pricing, and if they think it would be a good fit for you. Ask them to be brutally honest and listen with an open mind to their feedback.

Check the start-up costs. Start-up kits can range from $25 to more than $10,000. Compare the start up costs against what you could reasonably expect to earn. If the start-up kit costs $2800 and you earn 10% of total party sales, you'll have to sell $28,000 just to break even on your start-up kit. How many parties will that take? Will your kit need replenishing or supplementing, making it take even longer to begin earning cash? Finally, consider signing up as a representative for a number of companies with similar target audiences. You can do the work gaining customers and contacts once, but sell several products to your customer base.

Stay Up-to-Date

When do you plan on going back to work? The problems created by such a large gap on your resume can be minimized by staying current in your field. Attend seminars or courses when possible, and get involved in your industry's professional organization as a volunteer. This will demonstrate initiative and drive, and could be the difference between landing a good job or struggling to find one at all.

Flexible Work Arrangements

Back in the early 2000s, everyone was talking about how flexible work weeks would solve our work-life balance problems. Was the flexible work week just a fad? Yes and no. While few companies have implemented flexible options such as job sharing (two people share one job, working alternate days), many have implemented flextime programs for hours or days of work, or part time positions.

A dad who has to put in 40 hours a week at his office may choose to go in at 6:30 am while mom gets the kids off to school. By getting off around 3:00 pm he can pick the kids up from school, make dinner, and help with homework. If mom works four 10-hour days, she gets a three day weekend with the kids. Some companies may let you work remotely from home while on maternity leave and bank those hours for extra time off when you're back to work full-time. Be sure to check with Employment Insurance on the legality of any program your employer suggests—you don't want to get stuck paying back EI payments, along with penalties too. It may also prove to them that allowing you to work from home is beneficial to everyone—they keep a valuable employee satisfied and on the payroll while still getting the same amount of work done, and you get more face time with your kids, and a little more flexibility when something at home crops up.

There are many benefits to flexible work arrangements, and not just in favour of the employee. By introducing a flex arrangement, or accepting one, employers can prevent the loss of good employees. Morale and productivity generally improve while absenteeism decreases, and in the case of telecommuting, some costs can decrease significantly.

If your company doesn't have a flex program in place, you can still make an argument for them to create one for you. You'll need to create a proposal that outlines the benefits to the company, and your commitment to making it work. Creating this proposal will also help crystallize your thoughts on the matter—you may realize your job function simply won't work with a flexible arrangement.

When making your proposal, try to put yourself in the position of your employer. You need to make a strong business case for your request. How will the company benefit from this arrangement? Your boss? Your co-workers? Look into the history of flexible work arrangements with your company and department. Has it been tried in the past? Did it succeed or fail? Why? If your boss has had bad experiences with these types of arrangements, you'll have a harder time convincing him to take a chance on you.

Your proposal should be submitted in writing. Include what type of arrangement you're requesting (earlier or later hours, reduced hours, telecommuting, etc.). Address the impact on the business, and if you'll need to restructure your responsibilities in any way. Is this a permanent or temporary change? Clarify this point. What will the company gain from this arrangement? Anticipate and prepare for possible objections to your verbal presentation. Practice your presentation with a friend until you have answers to every question you could be asked, and have polished your delivery skills. You want to appear confident, not tentative or pessimistic.

Money Trap—Stay-at-Home Blahs

When you're pregnant, you're probably looking forward to escaping the rat race, and are imagining dreamy days lounging in bed with your cherubic new baby. No more scraping ice off the car windows before dawn, no more dressing up in pantyhose and suits, and no more struggling over whether or not to bring a lunch you know you won't eat because you invariably give in and go out for lunch with co-workers. While I'll admit that there were a few days that I didn't get out of my pajamas until I heard my husband's key in the door, more often than not I was up and raring to go, to get out of the house, to do something.

My husband thought he had a few years to go before he heard the first whiny, "I'm bored"—he definitely didn't expect it to come so soon and from me. It seemed I just needed more stimulation than a babbling baby could provide. I desperately needed to connect with other moms, but I couldn't afford to sign up for the many mom and tot classes available.

Whether you're a stay-at-home mom or dad, finding things to do that don't break your budget can be tough. It can also be hard to find new people to connect with, people that are also home during the day and have children your own children would like to play with.

Striking up a conversation with a stranger just because they have a baby with them isn't something everyone is comfortable initiating. Instead, turn to the Internet. People find the love of their life on the Internet—so why not find a friend for life? A local online community can provide a place for stay-at-home parents to get together both online and off.

On my first maternity leave, I assumed the only playgroups around were the ones that cost a lot of money in fees. However, I've since discovered that free or inexpensive community playgroups are abundant in most cities. Some of these groups are run by local health regions or family services offices, or simply are collectives of moms, requiring volunteering commitment rather than registration fees. Websites such as <**www.canadianparents.ca**> offer listings of mom and baby playgroups. You can join a group in your neighbourhood or start your own and find members through the website.

Many parents don't join a playgroup because they're unsure of what kinds of other people they'll encounter. You'll definitely find difference in groups. At one playgroup, the silence might be deafening—no one is really interested in getting to know the others. In another group, the chatter might be deafening, and regular playgroups can evolve into evening dinners, walks in the park, or nights out on the town, leaving the kids with a shared babysitter.

After Sera had her first son, Matthew, she found mom groups to be very supportive. "I was so overwhelmed with how my life changed after the birth of my son, and it was a huge comfort to meet with women who could relate to my situation." Now with three boys, Sera has different interests. "If anything, I crave the company of my childless friends where we hang out and not talk about kids the whole time!" she laughs. She recommends leaving the baby with Dad to reconnect with your girlfriends. "You come back with a renewed energy, ready to tackle the challenges of motherhood," she says.

Two Incomes and No Guilt—It *is* Possible

When I was three-years-old, my mom pulled me out of daycare to stay home with her and my new little brother. Guess what? Apparently I pitched a fit. I wanted to be at daycare with my friends, not home with mom.

There are many child care arrangements that might actually be much better for the child than staying home with mom. If mom spends all of her time cleaning and cooking, the child may not get the interaction he craves, and could begin acting out for attention. In a good daycare that has other children his own age and scheduled activities, he may thrive. At eight months, Kate couldn't tell me if she liked being at the home-based daycare all day. But on her second day there, she leaned out of my arms to reach for the owner at drop off-time. I knew she was enjoying it.

Recommended Surfing

*Having a hard time finding a family-friendly employer? Check out <**www.connectmoms. com**> for Canadian job listings posted by companies interested in the mom workforce.*

Tips for Balancing Work and Children

Following are some tips to assist you in achieving a happy balance between your work and home life, but if you're willing to change your job, you could look for an employer known for their family-friendly policies. *Today's Parent* magazine offers an annual list of the top ten family-friendly employers. These companies make the grade for offering benefits such as subsidized daycare, maternity or paternity top up, scholarship programs, flexible work arrangements, and even adoption funding.

- **Have a backup plan.** There will be nights when you have to work late, or days when your child is sick. Have a backup plan for a family member or friend (be sure to arrange ahead of time for this individual to have permission) to pick the child up from daycare or school and stay with them. When your child is sick, see if you can work from home, or have a friend or relative who can accommodate your sick child on short notice if you cannot leave work.
- **Stay organized**. A large, decorative square basket sits in the corner of the kitchen, collecting newspapers so they don't clutter the kitchen table all week. Grab and go snacks fill a designated drawer in the pantry to reduce time rummaging for something to throw in the lunch bags. Labelled bins by the front door hold hats, gloves, outdoor toys and shoe cleaning supplies. Where do you lose time everyday? Where does your frustration level start to rise? Organize your home to speed up the routine tasks so you can slow down and enjoy the fun stuff.
- **Ask for help**. Even a three-year-old can pick up their toys or grab themselves a snack of yogourt and an apple. If you have children old enough to do chores, determine what needs to be done and who (other than you) could be doing it. This teaches invaluable lessons about responsibility and household contributions. Don't expect or wait for help to be offered—ask for it! Children even younger than three may be able to help with some tasks—just expect it to take a little longer.

From the time my children were five-years-old they helped me bake and prepare meals. By the time Jack was 10, he was making homemade pizza for dinner once a week. Laura has been making quiche since she was nine. It's great knowing that once or twice a week, I don't have to cook dinner.

Joan, mom of two

Keep in mind that sometimes little helping hands can create more work than they complete—plan what they help with accordingly!

- **Be prepared**. You know mornings are hectic, so get things ready the night before. Ask the kids to choose their breakfast cereal and put out bowls and spoons. Make their lunches with them (also a great way to encourage eating those lunches). Try meal planning—it saves time and money.

- **Say no**. Establish your priorities. Create goals and only agree to things that match those goals. Is your goal to spend more time with your kids? Skip the drinks after work. Trying to carve out time for yourself? Committing to things you don't want to do leads to stress and feelings of hostility. And while saying no means that the individual requesting your time will be disappointed initially, they'll find someone else who can do whatever it is they were asking you to do. If you take the non-confrontational route and cancel at the last minute, it's a major blow to their project or feelings. Write down important events in your children's lives (school plays, church concerts) and treat them with the reverence they deserve, working your job around them.

- **Don't sweat the small stuff**. You've got an hour. Do you spend it dusting, or baking cookies with your daughter? (They don't have to be from scratch—boxed mixes count!) Do you go out to the backyard to play in the sand with your son, or scrub the bathroom? Sometimes, the right thing to do is to ignore the dust and leave the dishes in the sink overnight. There will always be plenty of chores and responsibilities, so relax your standards on the things you "should" do. I remember once asking my husband to bring in more garbage bags from the garage. He brought in a handful of bags and set them on the counter above the overflowing garbage and wandered off to play with the baby. Not only did he not put the bags under the cupboard where they usually go, but he didn't clue in that he could use one of the bags to replace the full one! He has a finely tuned filter when it comes to household chores, and he always chooses the kids first. If I always followed his lead our house would be unlivable, but in this regard he does have it right when it comes to child-centred prioritizing.

Going Out on Your Own—to Work!

Even in university I knew I wanted to run my own business one day. After Kate's birth, I got serious about trying to figure out exactly what I wanted to do, and when I wanted to do it. I wrote business plans for a number of different businesses, and I intended that within a year or two we could have our second child and after that maternity leave, start my own business.

At least, that was the plan. I chose to accept an offer to return to work early in order to get us ahead financially by a few extra months, but it did mean giving up some of that precious maternity leave. We didn't share our plans with many friends. Subsequently, when a co-worker discovered that I'd be returning to work four months before my maternity leave was up, she assumed I had been given a huge raise and was lured back with dollar signs in my eyes. "I wouldn't give up this time no matter how much they offered me—I love my baby too much," she said. I felt like I had been slapped. Surely she didn't mean to imply that I didn't love my child more than anything else, including money? Maybe I attributed too much maliciousness to the speaker. But it hurt, and I started to second-guess my decision.

I stayed on, and it seemed my co-worker wasn't the only one who was quick to judge my motives. "Couldn't resist the pay cheque, eh?" they'd joke. I quickly developed a thick skin, and focused on my ultimate goal— to someday have more flexibility and time for my children by giving up some of those things now. Within a week of going back to work, I decided not to wait a year or two—I wanted to start the business, a children's consignment store, right away.

I threw myself into planning and signed a lease, one that would see me open just weeks shy of my daughter's first birthday. I had an overwhelming amount of work—completing the interior construction of the store space (including hiring contractors for heating, electrical, plumbing, flooring and more), creating store policies and procedures, marketing and advertising, networking, sourcing and ordering inventory. I kept Kate in day care until two weeks after I had opened, and then switched her to part-time, bringing her into work with me a few days a week. Unfortunately, that wasn't feasible for my business or for her, so I returned her to full time to daycare, and began working 70 to 80 hours a week, letting my husband pick up all the slack at home, and be a single parent to Kate on evenings and weekends.

In opening and running a business that has quickly become successful by every measure, I've learned so much about the ups and downs of entrepreneurship that I'm often approached by other moms wanting to know how they can go into business for themselves and be successful and profitable. If you're considering joining the ranks of the self-employed, the next section should give you a starting point for discussion with your partner.

Bricks and Mortar Business

In the business world, particularly in retail, business owners often get asked if they are "bricks and mortar," meaning, do they have a physical location, or are they web-based? A children's consignment store, women's athletic shoe store, children's play centre, specialty coffee shop, independent bookstore, hair styling salon, fast food franchise—these are all bricks and mortar businesses. You leave your home to go to these businesses, there is inventory on the shelves, and you can't make money unless someone is there serving people.

Is opening a bricks and mortar business right for you? A hair stylist who opens a salon in her home can decide not to accept appointments on Thursdays, and while it will impact her business (what about clients who only have Thursdays available for personal errands?) it likely won't sink it, unless she creates too many similar restrictions. A bricks and mortar store, on the other hand, will be crippled if you make similar decisions, such as closing up every day at 3:30 pm to collect your kids from school.

A mom selling candles through home parties part-time who decides to change to a different product line may get stuck with display stock. As a consequence, her family members might receive candles every birthday for years to come. Alternatively, she can clear out her stock at cost on websites which sell used goods. In contrast, an art gallery owner who decides to quit could be stuck with paying out the balance of a four year lease and liable for a $80,000 bill for rent.

Here is where you must realize the difference between having a business and having a job. If you have a handyman business and you are the only handyman, then you have a job, with yourself as the boss. You trade the headache of working for someone else with the hassle of running your own job—handling the accounting, payroll, and marketing.

Entrepreneurship: The Road to Riches?

Let's say you were making $30,000 at your regular job, and decided you wanted to open a cooking school operating out of a small retail space. You invest $80,000 in the business to get it up and running, and aren't able to take any money out the first year—every dollar you bring in goes to pay for operations, investing in upgrades, attracting more customers through advertising, etc. In your second year, you manage to trim expenses and increase sales, and take out $15,000. Year three? Things are going well, and you take $25,000 home. Finally, in your fourth year, you take home a $40,000 pay cheque.

While you're making more than you did previously, in this scenario you have finally, after four years, paid yourself back the money you invested (money that could have been earning you interest). You'll also have "lost" $120,000 in wages you would have made had you kept working at your old job, plus whatever salary increases you might have received. Even if you manage to take out double your previous salary after four years, it will still be a few more years before you make back that lost income. What about benefits? If you're self-employed, you'll have to pay steep prices to get good coverage, and even then you may not get anywhere near the benefits you may have once had. No vacation pay either!

Of the many small businesses that fail in their first or second year (and 45% of Canadian businesses do), not all of them failed because they weren't profitable—some just weren't sufficiently profitable enough to be worth the work involved. Many small business owners decide that a reliable salary is more important than they originally thought or that the work involved in keeping the business successful is more than they want to undertake. Often businesses fail just as they're on the brink of success because they're undercapitalized.

Final Thought

Whether one of you decides to stay at home with the kids or you both work, know that you're making the decision that's right for you and your family, and no one has the right to make negative comments on that decision. That includes yourself. Don't be one of those people that says to parents who made different choices, "I just don't want strangers raising my children," or "I guess I just needed more intellectual stimulation that I got at home full-time." Many parents who both work are not doing it just to afford the luxuries of life—they're doing it to put food on the table and the clothes on their kids' backs.

CHAPTER FOUR

Navigating Government Benefits

THERE ARE A VARIETY OF different government programs in place to help families in Canada. However, these programs change from year to year. With each budget will come new programs, program cancellations, and changes to eligibility and levels of benefits. For the most up-to-date information on various government programs and benefits to parents, visit <**www.servicecanada.gc.ca**>.

Maternity and Parental Leave

Canada has a better than average national parental leave program, when you compare us with other industrial nations. Some countries, such as the United States, offer pathetic programs. Their *Family Medical Leave Act* (FMLA) only covers mothers for 12 weeks of unpaid leave with guaranteed job security (except in smaller companies). Some states do offer more comprehensive maternity leave options than others, just as some companies may offer extended benefits.

Some countries offer parental benefits that we can only dream about. In Sweden, for example, a mother is eligible for 16 months of parental leave split between herself and her partner, while still receiving 80% of her pay.

In Canada, we fall somewhere in the middle. While some companies offer top up programs for income, or extended leaves with job security, most working mothers will only receive basic maternity benefits, which fall under Canada's Employment Insurance program. These benefits are paid to birth mothers and surrogate mothers for up to 15 weeks. To receive maternity benefits you must have worked for 600 hours (about 15 weeks full time) in the last 52 weeks or since your last claim.

The mother can begin collecting maternity benefits a few weeks before the birth of the baby, but benefits end 17 weeks after the baby is born or the expected due date, whichever is later. If your baby is hospitalized, this 17-week window may be extended—the payments are not extended, just the deadline by which they can be collected.

As with maternity benefits, to receive parental benefits you have to have worked for 600 hours in the last 52 weeks or since your last claim. Parental benefits can be collected by either the biological or adoptive parents for up to a maximum of 35 weeks. These benefits can be claimed by one parent or shared between the two partners, but cannot exceed a combined maximum of 35 weeks. Parental benefits must be claimed within the 52 weeks following the child's birth, or for adoptive parents, within the 52 weeks from the date the child is placed with you. If your baby is hospitalized, this 35 week window may be extended.

In 2009, both maternity and parental leave payments were capped at 55% of your average insured earnings up to a yearly maximum insurable amount of $42,300. This places the current maximum payment at $447 per week. You could receive a higher benefit rate if you are in a low-income family. Your payment is a taxable income, meaning federal and provincial or territorial taxes will be deducted.

Sickness Benefits

If the mother experiences complications related to the birth of a child, she may be eligible for sick leave in addition to maternity leave. Sickness benefits may be paid up to 15 weeks to a person who is unable to work because of sickness, injury or quarantine. Mom must meet the 600 hours worked in the last 52 weeks or since her last claim requirement, and a doctor's note will be required. She could receive up to a maximum of 65 weeks of combined sickness, maternity and parental benefits instead of the normal combined maximum of 50 weeks. Often, sick leave is used in cases where the mother is confined to bed rest for pregnancy-related complications, or she has other pregnancy-related issues that prevent her from working.

Self-Employed

In 2010, the government introduced the *Fairness for the Self-Employed Act*. Previously, self-employed Canadians were not eligible for maternity or parental leave benefits. With an estimated 900,000 self-employed women in Canada, this was clearly an important issue. Under the new legislation, self-employed Canadians can now receive similar benefits to other employed Canadians if they opt into the program at least one year prior to claiming benefits and are responsible for making premium payments starting with the tax year in which they opt in to the program. The self-employed pay the same premium rate that salaried employees currently pay. They are not required to pay the employer's portion of the premium rate, as they do not have access to EI regular benefits. Self-employed workers can opt out of the program at the end of any tax year, as long as they have never received benefits.

A Little Something on the Side

Working while on leave can be a good way to earn extra money, whether it'll be used for making ends meet, paying for those extra baby sign language classes, or starting or topping up an RESP. It doesn't make financial sense to work while on the maternity portion of the benefit, as your earnings will be deducted dollar for dollar from your benefits. However, there might be circumstances where you benefit professionally from working a bit while receiving maternity benefits.

If you work while you're receiving parental benefits, you're allowed to earn $50 per week or 25% of your weekly benefits, whichever is higher. If you're receiving the maximum $447 per week, then you can earn just over $110 a week in additional income. Any income earned above that amount will be deducted dollar for dollar from your benefits.

Until December 4, 2010, the government is running a pilot project that increases the amount you can earn while working part-time and receiving maternity and parental benefits by allowing you to earn the greater of $75 or 40% of weekly benefits.

You must report any earnings you make while collecting maternity, sickness or parental benefits, which can be done either by phone or through written reports. It's relatively easy, and if you can work this small amount without paying child care costs, you're ahead of the game.

Canada Child Tax Benefit (CCTB)

The CCTB is a tax-free monthly payment made to eligible families with children under the age of 18. Included with the CCTB is the National Child Benefit Supplement (NCBS), a monthly benefit for low-income families with children. Family net income is one of the factors used in the calculation of your CCTB.

To obtain the CCTB, you must live with the child, you must be the person who is primarily responsible for the care and upbringing of the child, you must be a resident of Canada, and you or your spouse or common-law partner must be a Canadian citizen, a permanent resident, a protected person, or a temporary resident who has lived in Canada for the previous 18 months. To receive the CCTB, you must file an income tax and benefits return.

National Child Benefit Supplement (NCBS)

As noted above, the National Child Benefit Supplement (NCBS) is one part of the Canada Child Tax Benefit. It provides extra support to low-income families with children by topping up the monthly payments they receive under the CCTB system.

Universal Child Care Benefit (UCCB)

The UCCB is a $100 monthly payment designed to help Canadian families by providing direct financial support for child care arrangements for each child under the age of six years. Your child does not need to be in child care to receive this payment. The UCCB is taxable income, and you have to report it as income. To receive the UCCB, you do not have to have filed an income tax and benefits return, but you must complete an Application for Canada Child Benefits form. In the case of spouses and common-law partners, the UCCB payments are taxable in the hands of the spouse or common-law partner with the lower net income, regardless of which spouse or common-law partner received the payments. You'll get the paperwork for this program automatically from the hospital or your midwife, but it can take up to 80 days from the date of application for the money to start coming.

Family Supplement

The Family Supplement is a feature of Employment Insurance (EI) that provides additional benefits to low-income families with children. You do not have to apply for it. If you are eligible, your entitlement will automatically be added to your Employment Insurance payment.

If you or your spouse receives the Canada Child Tax Benefit (CCTB), then you are eligible to receive the EI Family Supplement on your family net income up to and including $25,921 per year.

The Family Supplement rate is based on your family net income and the number and age of the children in the family. The maximum Family Supplement will reach as high as 80% of your average insurable earnings. If you or your spouse claim Employment Insurance benefits at the same time, only one of you can receive the Family Supplement. Usually, it would be better for the spouse with the lower benefit rate to receive the Family Supplement.

Provincial Programs

Various provinces may have additional benefits, bonuses, or deductions for certain expenses, such as the two outlined below. If you're making a big decision such as quitting work to be a stay-at-home parent, it might be worth your while to meet with an accountant to talk about the specific programs available to you before you hand in your resignation. Also, keep in mind that all programs are subject to change over time—you may qualify for a supplement one year and not the next if the criteria for qualification are changed. The following are examples of two provincial programs.

British Columbia Basic Family Bonus

The B.C. Family Bonus program includes the Basic Family Bonus and the B.C. Earned Income Benefit. This program provides non-taxable monthly payments to help low- and modest-income families with the cost of raising children under the age of 18. The Basic Family Bonus provides a benefit of up to $111 per child per month when combined with the National Child Benefit Supplement. Benefits are calculated based on the number of children in the family and the family's net income. Families whose earned income is more than $3,750 a month may also be entitled to the B.C. Earned Income Benefit.

Ontario Child Benefit (OCB)

The OCB goes to all eligible low-income families with children from birth to age 18, whether they are working or receiving social assistance. Eligible families receive up to a maximum of $92 per child every month.

Write 'em Off—Tax Deductions

Canada Child Tax Credit

This federal non-refundable tax credit is for dependent children under the age of 18. When the child lives with both parents, the credit may be claimed by either spouse, with the unused portion transferable to the other spouse or common-law partner. In 2009, this amount was just over $2,000 per child. Some provinces offer a similar credit.

Children's Fitness Tax Credit

Gymnastics, art classes, music lessons, swimming, soccer, hockey, ballet—the list of classes and lessons you can sign up your children for is astonishing. While they all seem vital to having a well-rounded child, many parents make the decision to choose certain activities over others based on their eligibility for the Children's Fitness Tax Credit.

In 2007, the Government of Canada introduced a Children's Fitness Tax Credit for children. This tax credit allows a non-refundable tax credit based on eligible fitness expenses paid by parents to register a child in a prescribed program of physical activity. Parents may claim up to $500 per year for eligible fitness expenses paid for each child who is under 16 years of age at the beginning of the year in which the expenses are paid. The children's fitness tax credit is calculated by multiplying the total expense by the lowest marginal tax rate, not your actual tax rate.

An eligible fitness expense must be for the cost of registration or membership of a child in a physical activity program. Generally, such a program must be ongoing (either a minimum of eight consecutive weeks long or, for children's camps, five consecutive days long), be supervised, be suitable for children, and include a significant amount of physical activity that contributes to cardio-respiratory endurance, plus one or more activity that contributes to muscular strength, muscular endurance, flexibility, or balance. The organization you're considering will be able to tell you if they are eligible for the credit, and they will determine the part of the fee that qualifies for the tax credit. You must request a receipt for tax purposes.

Child Care Expenses Deduction

The maximum amount you're permitted to claim under the Child Care Expenses Deduction is $7,000 for each child under seven at the end of the year, and $4,000 for each child over seven and under 16. If both spouses are working, the lower-income earner must claim the deductions. If the lower-income earner is a full-time student, the deduction is available to the higher earner for the number of weeks the spouse attends school.

Learning Disabilities

Does your child have a confirmed or suspected learning disability? Learning disabilities range in severity and may interfere with the acquisition and use of oral language, reading, writing, or mathematics. If you suspect your child of having a learning disability, you can seek professional help in the form of psychological assessment by a registered educational psychologist. If your child has been diagnosed with a learning disability, you will be able to take advantage of deductions under the Medical Expense Tax Credit. Eligible deductions include tutoring services, transportation expenses (if over 40 kilometers), fees for specialized camps and private school tuition, talking textbooks and note taking services.

The Learning Disabilities Association of Canada <**www.ldac-acta. ca**> is an excellent resource for researching the various implications of having a child with a learning disability. This organization can help you understand how to best meet your child's needs, and can give you information to provide to your tax advisor to ensure you apply for all relevant deductions.

Final Thought

Every province has their own unique programs and subsidies to help parents pay for child care, after school activities and other expenses. You can often find a lot of information from your local child services office, by spending some time online browsing local parenting resource sites, or by talking to other more experienced parents.

CHAPTER FIVE

Preparing for the Future

BECOMING A PARENT MEANS YOU have to learn about a lot of things very quickly, and I don't just mean learning about the merits of cloth vs. disposable diapers, or debating discipline styles with your spouse. Previously, when you had no helpless beings depending on you, you probably didn't think much about life insurance, wills, and emergency savings accounts. Well, now it's time!

Call the Lawyers—Creating Your Will

For most parents, the birth of their first child underscores all previous realizations—that life is both precious and fragile. Where once you didn't hesitate to spend your weekends engaging in fun but risky pastimes, now you may find yourself thinking, "What if I get hurt? What will happen to the kids?"

What will happen to your kids if you die before they turn 18? What will happen to you, and to them, if you're incapacitated? When you die, what happens to your estate—your property and savings?

As a responsible parent, these are questions you need to be able to answer, and they can be answered by writing your will. A will and the corresponding estate plan is one of the most important documents for all families. Without a valid will, existing provincial legislation (called the intestacy rules) would apply to determine the administration of the estate and the distribution of the property. This would also mean that the deceased parent would have no input into the guardianship of the minor children, and the children would have to wait to receive their portion of the deceased's estate until they reach the age of 18. Furthermore, without a will there is no opportunity for tax planning and no discretion over the administration of the will.

As you can imagine, the most important issue is the guardianship of your children. Do you want one of the grandparents to receive guardianship? If so, which one? Alternatively, would you prefer one of your siblings or friends to assume responsibility? What about your eldest child? If they're 18 when you die, are they sufficiently responsible to raise their younger siblings? You'll want to consider these questions carefully. Potential guardians should be able to handle the financial burden your children represent, provide parenting consistent with your values, and be able to maintain the children's quality of life, such as keeping them in the same school rather than uprooting them and moving them across the country. If you have life insurance, the children may receive an enormous sum of money upon your death—a will stipulates who will control this money to help ensure it is used responsibly.

Parents on a budget may be tempted to use a generic will kit for under $40, available at office supply stores and bookstores. However, a will created using a kit cannot offer the same protection as a properly executed estate plan. If your will causes any disagreement among remaining family members with an interest in the estate and the welfare of your children, such as grandparents disagreeing with your choice of guardian, there are many more opportunities to find small errors, or inconsistencies with a will created using a kit. Even the smallest error can result in the will being found invalid and tossed out, at which point your estate will be treated as though you had no will at all. If this happens, or if you didn't have a will at all, the surviving parent could be left with no access to life insurance payments or a separately-owned bank account for months while the paperwork is sorted out.

You will require professional assistance to prepare your will. Look for a lawyer with whom you feel comfortable, and who offers a wills and estate service as part of their practice. They will guide you through the preparation process, providing you with planning options and various opportunities based on your current circumstances and possible future scenarios. You can expect to pay between $300 and $750 for a professionally prepared estate plan.

An estate plan is one of those expenses of parenting that offer no tangible rewards unless a tragedy occurs. It's difficult to part with the money for an estate plan when what your "estate" really needs is a new vacuum cleaner or school fees. Shop around for a good price and ensure your plan covers as many plausible scenarios as you can think of to avoid frequent, costly revisions.

Assurance Through Insurance

Home, automobile and life insurance are designed to protect you from unforeseen loss or injury that you otherwise could not afford to repair on your own. This means that if your transmission breaks down on your car as a result of poor maintenance, your insurance won't cover the cost of its repair. However, if you're in a serious car accident and your car is written off, so long as you have the appropriate insurance, you'll receive a cheque. If you simply get a dent in your bumper, while your insurance may technically cover it, it may be smarter to pay for the repair yourself, rather than have the black mark on your claims record.

These Four Walls

The media frequently reports sad stories about people who have had house fires or robberies and lost everything. Sometimes charitable organizations or family members step in to help, or a local business will start a collection. Most of the time, whatever money is raised is only enough to help the family buy enough food and clothes to last a few weeks, or rent a hotel room until they can find another place to live.

What would happen to you if your home burnt down? Where would you live? How could you afford to replace your posessions? Could you afford to continue to stay home with your kids, or return to the same standard of living?

If you're a renter, in case of a fire or burglary, the landlord may have insurance on the property, but he won't have coverage for its contents— your possessions. You'll need to purchase renters insurance to protect yourself and your belongings.

If you own your own home, insurance is more costly, and even more important. In fact, if you haven't paid off your home yet, you'll probably already have house insurance, as proof of insurance is required by mortgage brokers and banks before they'll approve you for a mortgage.

Vroom, Vroom—Automobile Insurance

Though insurance programs, requirements and rates vary from province to province, Canadians must maintain a minimum level of insurance on their vehicles in the event of an accident that damages property or injures or kills a third party. The current minimum third party liability is $1,000,000. However, in these days of rising costs and higher settlements, it may be wise to purchase third-party liability insurance with up to $2,500,000 in coverage.

Basic third party liability insurance covers the damage to another person's vehicle or settlements for their injuries or loss of life, but not your own. For your own coverage, you require physical damage insurance, which includes collision, comprehensive, or both. Many people waive this coverage to save money, as it can be expensive. In some provinces though, this coverage is so also mandatory. If you negotiated a bank loan to purchase your car, or are leasing the vehicle, your bank or leasing agency may require you to purchase this comprehensive insurance. Fire and theft insurance is usually covered under third party liability polices—be sure to check.

The coverage on your own vehicle generally requires you to pay a deductible when making a claim. The higher the deductible you are willing to pay, the lower your premiums. When making a claim, find out if there are specific circumstances in which the deductible would be waived.

Life and Disability Insurance

Why buy life or disability insurance? How will your family cover basic living expenses if one of you were to require around-the-clock care because of an accident or other disability? How would the surviving spouse pay for funeral expenses? What would happen to your childrens' standard of living without your income? If your spouse stays at home with the kids, his or her death will require you to cover at minimum the cost of child care. If your company doesn't offer extended leaves for grieving, you may find you're unable to return to work when you're required to, and having insurance for these eventualities gives you more flexibility.

A house painter doesn't get into his truck in the morning planning to be hit head on by a semi-trailer, spend the next nine months in the hospital recovering, and be discharged with a lifelong physical handicap that forces a complete career change, if not the end of their working career. A father of twin babies can't imagine taking a call telling him his wife had a brain aneurysm, then died on the way to the hospital, leaving him completely alone to parent newborn twins. A mom of three doesn't spend time thinking about what would happen if her husband was diagnosed with cancer and died a few short months later.

Who will pay for medical bills or prescriptions the government doesn't cover? How will you pay for full time nursing care if it is required? A grieving husband may find it impossible to go back to work when his bereavement leave expires, but knows he still has to provide for his children.

Before you go shopping for life and/or disability insurance, check with your employer. They may offer short or long-term group disability coverage, or life insurance, at no cost to you. You may be able to increase the extent of this coverage by paying an extra premium each month. If free coverage isn't offered, check to see if a company plan exists which you can buy into. While the entire cost will be yours to cover, a company plan rate could be significantly better than the cost of an individual plan though another insurance company.

When it comes to life insurance, there are two main choice—whole life and term. Term life insurance provides coverage at a fixed rate for a defined term, typically 5 to 10 years. Term life insurance is often inexpensive to begin with, but premiums will increase with age. However, you may not need term insurance when it's time for the premiums to increase; at this point you might have built up sufficient net worth so that the loss of a spouse's income will not affect your household to the same severity.

Whole life policies are very different from term policies. In a whole life policy, you agree to pay a monthly premium, which is applied against your policy. Once the policy is paid up, you can continue to pay the monthly premium. These excess payments are invested by the company and earn interest. If your investments perform well, your policy will have a higher cash value and death benefit. If the investments lose money, you'll have a lower cash value and death benefit. You can also take loans against the cash value of your policy, but if you don't pay them back with interest, your beneficiaries will receive a smaller death benefit. Some plans offer cash surrender options that allow you to cancel your policy and receive a lump sum tax-free payment.

You should reexamine your disability and life insurance needs whenever you experience major life changes—such as having more children, after a separation or divorce, or a loss or change of employment.

What it Costs

Insurers decide their insurance rates for home, car, life and disability insurance based on your risk factors, some of which are in your control, and some of which are not. Obviously, the higher your risk factors, the more expensive your insurance premiums.

Risk factors that are not in your control include your age, gender, medical history, type of home, distance from a fire hall, etc. Risk factors that are in your control include your hobbies (sky divers pay more than gardeners), insurance history, habits such as smoking, and to some degree, even your health. Among other things, if you have a basement suite, fireplace, alarm system or swimming pool your assessed level of risk will be higher.

Some companies offer discounts for holding multiple policies with them, such as home, automobile and life. It's a good practice to get at least three or four quotes before you decide to buy, and to choose the best price from a reputable company.

Home insurance is generally inexpensive unless you live in a rural area, or in a very nice home. Auto insurance can be a great deal more expensive, especially if you have a history of accidents, or are insuring teenage children on your policy. Life insurance has a large range of pricing. A 27-year-old non-smoking male looking for $1 million in coverage can expect to pay around $25 a month for a five-year term policy, while whole life insurance for the same individual might come in at $225 a month for 20 years.

Tips to Save on Insurance

- Shop around, and be sure to read the fine print. Make sure you're comparing apples to apples when it comes to what your policy covers.
- Switching companies? Don't cancel the policy by not paying the bill at renewal time. Instead, send a cancellation letter. Other insurers may consider your non-payment as defaulting, and your rates may increase.
- Another thing to consider when changing insurance companies is to do so only at renewal time. Much like cell phone providers, cancelling your coverage before the term ends may result in large penalties.
- When comparing rates, ensure the coverage is the same. A suspiciously low quote may reflect a restrictive policy that fails to provide coverage when you make a claim.
- Avoid making small claims. Too many claims on your record and your company will raise your rates, or drop your policy altogether. If this happens, you may be stuck buying facility insurance from companies with astronomical premiums.
- Never lie on your application form. If you claim to be a non-smoker and your house fire is caused by an improperly disposed of cigarette, you can be sure your insurance company will attempt to find proof that someone in the household smokes. If they can prove it, they can deny your claim.

Emergency Fund

Do you need an emergency fund? Some experts says that if you have debt (excluding your mortgage), it's more important to pay off the debt first, and then focus on savings—emergency fund first, then RRSPs, Tax Free Savings Account (TFSA), Registered Education Savings Programs (RESPs), etc. However, many families will carry consumer debt for much

Credit Balance Insurance

Are you paying credit balance insurance on your credit cards or loans? If you don't know, it's time to find out. This is yet another reason why it's important to review policies associated with your mortgage, credit cards, and loans carefully, and to check your statement monthly. You may find you're paying hundreds of dollars annually to cover tiny payouts. Generally, you'll pay far more for this insurance with a small potential payout than you will for proper disability or life insurance with a much bigger payout. The average cost of credit balance insurance is about $1 for every $100 balance. So if you carry a $4,000 balance, the insurance alone would cost $40 per month. If something happens and you need to make a claim, the payout is generally the minimum monthly payment on the debt for a defined period of time. For the same $40 a month you could probably buy a term life policy that would pay out the hundreds of thousands of dollars.

of their lifetime—if they wait to pay off their debt, an emergency fund will never become a priority. And simply having room on your line of credit doesn't cut it—for instance, if you need access to cash because of job loss, there are no guarantees your bank won't decrease your lending limit right when you need the money the most.

Earlier I mentioned Canadian financial expert Gail Vaz-Oxlade, and I'm going to recommend her again. Take a look at her personal website <www.gailvazoxlade.com> and spend some time reading the articles and blog posts there, and definitely bookmark the website so you never miss a blog post. She has written a great deal about the importance of having an emergency fund, and I think she sums up the need for one perfectly in this particular blog post.

Still No Emergency Fund? Really?

Reprinted by permission from Gail Vaz-Oxlade

I routinely meet people who do not have an emergency fund. And I hear from hundreds more; sad souls who have hit a wall and have no money to help them over. I'm not sure what else I can say to influence them to get this very important part of their financial safety net in order other than this: Caca Happens. If you have some money available to help you through, things will be a lot less stressful than if you're dealing with *caca* and *no money* at the same time.

It doesn't really matter how well you think things are going. Like the economy, life is a cycle. Sometimes you're on your way up the positive side. Sometimes you're on your way down the negative side. That's just the way life is. And it really shouldn't come as any surprise at all since it has always been thus.

Building up an emergency fund is an important part of your risk management. But you already know that. It's pretty standard advice from anyone who knows anything about money and life. Your mother gave you a version of this lesson when she encouraged you to tuck a twenty somewhere safe when you were going off on a date so if things didn't go well, you had the money to get home under your own steam. Your mother didn't tell you that? Hmmm.

Sticking a twenty somewhere safe is still good advice. Except a twenty doesn't really cut it when you have a $1,200 mortgage payment, a $300 car payment, kids to feed, a home to heat, and medical costs that have to be covered.

The biggest problem with not having an emergency fund is that when the caca does hit the fan you're going to go into debt, or deeper into debt, just to meet your most basic needs. So an emergency fund is also a safety net against more debt. And an emergency fund can help you smooth out your budgeting because when unexpected expenses hit your doorstep, you don't have to constantly be rejigging your budget to make it to the end of the month. You can use some of your emergency fund for the emergency, and keep your budget on track.

But Gail, I can hardly manage on the money I'm making now. Where am I supposed to get the money for an emergency fund?

Start small. If you don't have much to save, it doesn't matter—the important thing is just to start. Even if it's only $20 per paycheck, start. As long as you haven't started, you're not building your emergency fund. Once you've started, you're on your way and then it only becomes a matter of how to boost the amount you're setting aside.

To create your emergency fund, set up an automatic deduction from your regular account to a high-interest savings account. Whether you go with ING Direct™, The President, or your local credit union, find the account with the highest interest you can. Don't settle for some pathetic savings account being touted as an "investment account" from your local bank. You work hard for your money, and your money should work just as hard for you.

One of the best ways to establish an emergency account is with a payroll deduction at work. This is particularly true for all of you people who have no discipline! Employers often offer the option of deducting some money from each of your pays and putting that money in a savings bond. There. You won't even miss it since the money never hits your bank account. Of course you have to treat that money as sacred. If you pull the money out every time you "create a stupid emergency"—gee honey, we really do need a new front door—then you're playing a game with yourself, and you will *lose*!

Okay, once you've started your emergency fund, sticking away your $20, $30 or $50 a pay, you're on your way. But you can't pat yourself on the back just yet. Since the rule of thumb is that you need at least three months of essential emergency expenses set aside, you must find a way to boost your savings to reach your goal in a reasonable period of time.

One way is to reduce what you're spending in one category of your budget and send that money to your high interest savings account. Most people have things they can cut back on. Do you buy coffee every day on the way to work? Do you smoke? Do you pick up the latest magazine at the checkout counter? Do you subscribe to premium cable? Do you go out for a drink with your friends after work? Buy your lunch at work? Pick up your favourite "stuff" whenever it's on sale even though you already have 30 pairs of shoes, white shirts, handbags, DVDs, name your vice here.

One great tip I picked up from a regular visitor to the website is the Tit-for-Tat approach to savings. Each time this woman buys herself something she considers a *want*, she contributes an equal amount to her savings account. Not only does it make her really think about whether she's going to spend the money—because in essence whatever she buys is going to cost her cash flow twice as much—she's saving for the future while she enjoys her todays.

Assuming you've been working like a dog to get your debt paid off, once it is, don't just incorporate all that money back into your spending plan. Take 30% and use it to boost your emergency fund. (If you've already hit your emergency fund goal, use that 30% for long term savings.)

Debt free with a safety net? Rock-on!

Schooled—RESPs

Maybe it's the fact that you're still paying off your own student debt that makes you so determined to save for your child's education, or perhaps you want your kids to have more choice over where they attend school. Whatever your reason, you've probably decided to at least examine your options in saving for the future educational needs of your kids.

According to the 2008–2009 *Guide to University Costs in Canada* issued by USC Family Education Savings Plans Inc., a four-year degree at a Canadian university will cost nearly $97,600 by 2022. Incidental expenses, such as local travel, entertainment, phone, cable, utilities and household incidentals are included, at an estimated cost of $2,500 annually. Remove that cost from the equation and a student attending university and living at home will face a tuition and books bill of about $59,400 in 2022. Some estimates put a four-year program with residence costs included even higher, moving beyone $100,000 after 2023.

Will tuition really be that high? It could be. Yet, when I look back at my university days, I paid just under $4,000 a year for basic tuition. At the same school, it's now just under $5,000. In 10 years, it's only gone up by $1,000. That's a 25% jump, but over a 10-year period. Annually, the increase is just 2.5%. I wonder if the jump will really be as high as they say. For our family savings calculations, we're going to assume basic tuition for my kids will likely come in around $6,500 a year—or $26,000 for a four-year program.

Those are still frightening numbers, whether you have just one child or a whole hockey line. Though it would be nice if we could guarantee every one of our children a four-year university program free of charge, there are many factors to consider that make your individual family savings needs different.

Deciding how much to save for your children's education is like deciding how much to save for retirement; it's more art than science. Obviously you can't know in advance if your child will go to university, college or a technical school. Where they go to school counts too, because tuition varies wildly in schools across Canada. There are also living expenses to consider if your child decides to attend an out-of-town school, and those expenses vary from city to city and province to province.

Your own beliefs about education will come into play as well. In my first book, *Sink or Swim: Get Your Degree Without Drowning in Debt* (Dundurn, 2003), I recounted how I had very little financial assistance from my parents and still managed to graduate with almost no debt. In hindsight, I see that my struggles to balance school, work, and play were character-building and, in the end, were beneficial to my career as well. I'd like my children to struggle somewhat as well, but I'd also hate to see them deny themselves a good education because it's all too difficult.

Without knowing how much they'll need, what percentage you'll want to cover, and how the investment will perform, it's difficult to say how much money you should save every month. It may be better to consider how much you can afford to contribute, and how the government's contributions will affect the balance.

Yes, there are government contributions! A lot of people have heard about Registered Education Savings Programs (RESPs), but few understand how they work, and even fewer understand the benefits and pitfalls associated with them.

According to a 2005 poll commissioned by Investors Group to better understand investors' financial behaviour, almost half of Canadian parents have not saved enough to send their children to university for even one year. And 51% have not set up Registered Education Savings Plans for their children. According to the poll, even the parents who had set up a plan were often not making the most of them: 45% said they've saved less than $10,000 in RESPs.

So what exactly is an RESP? It's essentially a savings plan the government has created to help you help your children with their post-secondary education. When you contribute to the plan, the government kicks in 20% on top.

You can invest up to $50,000 per child in an RESP. There are no annual limits on RESPs. However, the Canada Education Savings Grant (CESG) portion (the 20% government portion based on the amount you contribute) will only be paid on the first $2,500 of contributions made every year, up to a lifetime maximum of $7,200 for each child. If you have accumulated unused grant room, then the Canada Education Savings Grant will be paid on the first $5,000 of contributions made per year. Low-income families receive a higher CESG rate on the first $500 contributed.

Contributions to an RESP are not tax-deductible. However, the money grows on a tax-deferred basis. The money is eventually taxed on the student's personal rate when withdrawn, and this will likely be lower than the parent's rate was at the time of contribution. Depending on their income level at the time they withdraw the funds, they may be withdrawing the money tax-free if their income is very low. Which is a key feature of this program. If the student is withdrawing the money in addition to earning income they could pay tax on the money withdrawn—effectively being taxed twice.

Your children will be able to withdraw the money from the RESP when they are enrolled full-time in a qualifying education program at a designated university, community college or junior college. The money can then be used to cover books, accommodation and tuition—basically anything that will help the student during their studies. A $5,000 limit is imposed for the first 13 weeks of a qualifying educational program, with no limits afterwards.

Some parents worry that if Junior decides against higher learning, their money is lost. Fear not—with most plans, if your teen decides to spend his days surfing in Tofino instead of pursuing a degree, you can transfer up to $40,000 into your RRSP. If you don't have room, you can cash out the funds (subject to a 20% penalty tax and the repayment of the government grant). If you have created a family plan with all of your children named as beneficiaries, the government's portion paid into the plan can be used by the other children named in the plan, up to a maximum of $7,200 per student. So if you have three children and only one goes on to pursue a post-secondary education, the student can utilize $7,200 of the CESG portion of the RESP—any CESG above this amount must be paid back.

If you choose to invest with your bank, the plan you set up is a self-directed plan. You choose where your money is invested. Your banker will guide you through the RESP creation process, as well as the application process for the Canada Education Savings Grant and any provincial grants. You can make deposits when you have the money available, or you can set up an automatic withdrawal system.

Watch Out! Group Education Savings Plans

You may have seen advertisements encouraging you to enter to win a $1,000 contribution towards your child's RESP, or been accosted at a parenting trade show by eager salespeople asking you if you want to win $500 towards your child's future education. Fill out the form and you're sure to have an education savings plan sales representative calling you day and night to set up an appointment to open a savings program for your child. That's because the salespeople work on commission, and often receive incentives for selling a certain number of plan units. A scholarship trust fund is a "pooled" or "group" plan. Your money is pooled with that of other parents and used to purchase plan units. When you are ready to withdraw money, you share in the pooled earnings of investors with children the same age as yours.

Pooled group plans have a spotty reputation. Generally, if you cancel your plan, need to change your contribution schedule, or your child does not go to school you could forfeit the plan earnings, the CESG and the fees. Combined with the fact that scholarship plans are often limited to investing in low risk, low return investments, it's entirely possible that after 20 years of contributions you'll receive less than what you contributed, not more. Group plans do not offer the same payout flexibility as self-directed plans. Pay-outs may be made annually or semi-annually until the schooling is completed.

Need a few more downsides? The fees might be ridiculously high, and not well publicized. There are enrolment fees, administration fees, investment management fees, depository fees, trustee fees and more. These fees are paid up front from your contributions. Plus, pooled group plans are riskier than individual plans because you have less flexibility in the way you make your payments. If you miss a contribution and your account goes into default, you could lose your earnings. Some plans impose far more restrictive regulations regarding what schools or types of post-secondary program actually qualify for pay-outs than you will experience with a basic RESP established by either your financial planner or financial institution.

When considering a group plan, remember that whether you choose a self-directed plan or a group plan, all RESP contributions are eligible for the Canada Education Savings Grant. The group plan funds have been the target of many formal consumer complaints. Some salespeople will go so far as to insinuate that the government-matching portion is only eligible to parents in their plan—not true! Any parent investing in a properly registered plan, including those organized through the bank, will receive the grant.

I strongly encourage you to do your own research and speak with your personal banker before signing any contract with a group fund. Choose a plan that offers flexibility, one where you can establish a regular contribution, but which can be changed if your financial situation changes, and one where you can make lump sum payments whenever you have them. Ask a lot of questions before you sign anything. We chose to set up a family RESP with non-scheduled contributions. All three children are named in one plan, so if one or more of the kids chooses not to pursue a qualified program, we don't have to worry about closing their individual RESP—the benefits are simply shared by the children that do qualify. Being self-employed in the retail business, I liked not being tied to a specific contribution each month, and instead having the flexibility to contribute lump sums when the business allows it.

Grandma's Cash Gifts

Where do you find the extra money needed for investing in RESPs? One place is those cheques you may receive for your child's birth, baptism, or birthdays. If relatives give money instead of gifts, it's easy to mentally earmark that money for their savings. When writing thank you notes, you can refer to the fact that the money has been invested, and how much you appreciate the giver's contribution.

You can deposit the money directly into their RESP accounts until they're old enough to start wanting the money themselves, at which point you can begin discussions about their money management.

Some parents make it a policy to invest any unexpected money that comes their way into their child's RESP. The Child Tax Credit, a tax refund, government rebate checks, performance bonuses, yard sale proceeds, cash from consigning your children's outgrown clothes and toys—these are all examples of "windfalls" not normally accounted for in your family budget that could be directed towards your child's RESP.

Trusts

Wealthy families that have significant assets often set up family trusts. Though these trusts are not eligible for the government's contributions, they can be used to split income with children and other family members in order to save on taxes. Family trusts also provide a way of providing multiple access to the capital gains deduction.

Recommended Surfing

Canada Education Savings Grant (CESG)
<www.canlearn.ca>.

Saving for Your Future

Financial experts recommend that you ensure you've begun saving for your future before you worry about saving for your child's education. Others recommend that before you start saving for your retirement, you should consider paying off high-interest debt first. The information below provides a general overview of how RRSPs (Registered Retirement Savings Plans) work for you to start thinking about, whether you are ready to start investing now, or in the future.

How much do you need? The Canada Pension Plan (CPP) is intended to provide retirement income of about 25% of the average Canadian wage. Old Age Security (OAS) benefits are in addition to the CPP, bringing the number up to 40%. Remember though, this is 40% of the average Canadian wage, just over $40,000 at the time of printing. That's approximately $16,000—not exactly enough to guarantee a carefree retirement. However, if you're one half of a couple who are both receiving the maximum amount, and you have paid off your mortgage and debt, it certainly would be enough to survive.

Conventional retirement wisdom says you should have saved enough or accumulated enough assets to provide you with about 70% of your pre-retirement income. There is an assumption that you will own your own home with no mortgage, and have no outstanding loans. As you can see, there's a major gap between what the experts recommend, and what the government offers. That's where your savings come in, whether they're in the form of securities, real estate, RRSPs, TFSAs, or other items.

An RRSP is a plan registered with the Canada Revenue Agency that holds investments. Contributions are tax-deductible, and the gains grow tax-free until you make withdrawals from the plan, at which point they are taxed at your income tax rate at the time of withdrawal. Also, the amount you withdraw can affect your government benefits. Contributions are tax-deductible, meaning that they're valuable to those in higher tax brackets. According to Statistics Canada, barely a third of Canadians who are entitled to make an RRSP contribution do, and over the past few years, the total amount contributed was approximately 6% of what could have been.

I know you've heard it before, but it's wise advice: pay yourself first. If you wait every month to see how much money you can afford to put in, you likely won't contribute anything. Instead, set up an automatic bank withdrawal for the amount you'd like to contribute. This method also takes advantage of dollar-cost-averaging. Your contribution buys fewer shares when the price is high and more when the price is low. After a period of time, your average share price will probably be lower than if you had bought in with infrequent lump sum contributions.

Your financial advisor will offer suggestions as to what kinds of investments you should purchase, including GICs, mutual funds, bonds, stocks, etc. Individuals close to retirement with little savings may decide to invest in riskier stocks to maximize the potential for profit, or they may decide to play it safe and invest in low-interest options with guaranteed returns. A qualified advisor will determine your risk tolerance and make recommendations based on your tolerance for risk and savings goals.

At the time of printing, you can contribute up to 18% of your earned income from the previous year, up to a maximum of $21,000. Adjustments may be made depending on any pension plans you have, and your carry-forward of unused RRSP contribution room since 1991. To determine your contribution limit, check your last year's Notice of Assessment. If you have a very high contribution limit, you can get an RRSP loan from your bank. Many people do this shortly before the tax deadline of March 1. You apply the entire loan to your RRSP, and receive the tax refund shortly after. You apply the tax refund to the loan, then begin paying off the balance of the loan. Even with the interest you pay on the loan it's still a good deal, especially so if you hadn't previously been saving anything at all. However, if you have the discipline to pay back a loan, you may have the discipline to simply set up an automatic withdrawal from your bank account to begin building an RRSP investment.

You can continue to contribute to an RRSP until the end of the calendar year in which you turn 71 as long as you're still earning income, at which time you must convert your RRSP into a Registered Retirement Income Fund (RRIF), buy an annuity, or withdraw it in cash, depending on your financial situation and how much you have saved. If your spouse is younger than you, you can contribute to a spousal RRSP.

RRSPs can be very important for young families who have not yet purchased their first home. Though money removed from your RRSP will be taxed at your current income tax rate, you can withdraw tax-free under two programs, although you have to pay this money back into your RRSP over time. First-time homebuyers are permitted to withdraw up to $20,000 from their RRSPs as a down payment on a home. You have 15 years to repay the money back into your RRSP, and of course, the money you pay back is not tax-deductible.

Those interested in going back to school are permitted to withdraw up to $20,000 from their RRSPs to defray tuition costs under the Lifelong Learning Plan (LLP). You have 10 years to repay the money back into your RRSP. Again, repayments are not tax deductible.

The truth is, you can withdraw money from your RRSP at any time, for any reason. Common reasons to do this include job loss, entrepreneurship, or even deciding to take a year off to travel. In these three scenarios you would experience a lower income, so the money you withdraw would be taxed, but at a lower rate than if you were still working full time. However, you are not permitted to pay back these withdrawals—so the withdrawn contributions are gone forever, as is the interest those investments would have earned.

Spousal RRSPs

If yours is a one-income family, or a two-income family with a large discrepancy in salary between the two earners, spousal RRSPs can be a vital part of your investment strategy. The higher earning spouse will contribute to a spousal RRSP as a way to reduce the family's overall tax bill. The same amount of income is taxed at a lower rate or not at all if the lower income earner's income is low enough. Common-law relationships are also eligible for spousal RRSPs.

There is a three year attribution rule to keep in mind. It's designed to prevent a high-income spouse from simply contributing to a spousal RRSP and having the lower-income spouse turning around and withdrawing the cash at a lower income tax rate immediately. If your spouse withdraws from their spousal RRSP within three calendar years of your last contribution to any spousal RRSP, the withdrawal is treated as income on your personal tax return. If the withdrawal is made more than three years after the contribution, the withdrawal is treated as income on your spouse's tax return. The three year rule does not apply if both individuals are living apart due to the breakdown of a marriage, the contributing spouse has died in the year a withdrawal is made, or either spouse becomes a non-resident of Canada for tax purposes.

Hiring a Financial Advisor

Even if you have very little to invest, the services of a good financial advisor are invaluable. In addition to managing your investments, a financial advisor can provide debt counseling, investment strategies, and assistance with your family budget.

Before you start looking for an advisor, gather your financial records and have a discussion with your partner about your financial goals. Borrow easy-to-understand financial planning books from the library, such as David Bach's *Smart Couples Finish Rich* or his *Automatic Millionaire* series, to learn the lingo and have a basic understanding of financial planning.

Choosing a financial advisor at random using the Yellow Pages is not a good idea. You want someone reputable and someone with whom you can work with a sense of comfort and ease. You can ask friends or family for a referral, or ask a professional you respect, such as your company's lawyer or your doctor. Only select an advisor who has a professional designation, as they must abide by certain rules and regulations, including a code of ethics. Do not use a "friend of a friend" who's taking a financial planning class at the local community college. For a complete list of designations, and additional information on selecting a financial advisor, visit <**www. advocis.ca/content/consumers/designations.html**>.

You should interview at least three advisors, asking them about their education, experience, areas of specialization, and investment principles. You'll also want to discuss how frequently you'll communicate, and how their fees are structured.

After your initial conversation, you should have a good gut feeling about whether you'd trust this person, and would enjoy working with them. Now it's time to do your own version of a background check on them. Request references from clients, both current and former. If the advisor has partnerships with other professionals (such as insurance brokers) ask for a reference from a partner as well. You can also call their professional associations to ensure they are a member in good standing.

Your financial advisor's compensation can eat into the money you have allotted for investing. Advisors are compensated by commissions or fees, or variations of the two.

In a commission-only arrangement, your advisor earns commissions generated on transactions. In a fee-only arrangement, you pay the advisor a set rate, often hourly. Some advisors charge an annual fee based on a sliding scale. They may charge 1% to 2% of assets annually to create and oversee the portfolio, plus the management fees on the funds.

One of the least expensive methods of investing is to pay for the initial establishment of your portfolio, and you can take over the management thereafter. The advisor would help you choose investments based on your tolerance for risk.

Tax-Free Savings Accounts (TFSA)

In 2008, the Canadian government launched a new program of Tax-Free Savings Accounts (TFSA). It's a flexible savings plan that allows Canadians to contribute up to $5,000 a year to the account, and investment income, including capital gains earned within the account will not be taxed and withdrawals will be tax-free.

Unlike RRSPs, contributions to TFSAs are not tax deductible. Like RRSPs, unused room can be carried forward. Capital gains and other investment income earned in a TFSA will not be taxed. Neither income earned within a TFSA nor withdrawals from it will affect eligibility for federal income-tested benefits and credits (such as the Canada Child Tax Benefit, the GST credit, the Age Credit, and Old Age Security and Guaranteed Income Supplement benefits). Withdrawals will create contribution room for future savings. The $5,000 annual contribution limit will be indexed to inflation in $500 increments.

So if you have cash to invest, what's better—a TFSA or a RRSP? There's no easy answer, and it's something best discussed with your financial advisor. As a general rule of thumb, if you think the money you're saving will truly not be touched until your retirement, the RRSP option is likely a better option. Also, if you're in a high income bracket and are contributing a large sum to savings, the RRSP may also be the better choice. However, if you're looking for something with lots of flexibility, the TFSA is likely your best choice.

Want to really get into the nitty gritty of which program is better before you seek expert advice? Check out <**www.taxtips.ca/calculator/ tfsavsrrsp.htm**> and play with their TFSA vs. RRSP calculator.

Final Thought

I hope this chapter has convinced you that it's time to bring in the professionals. When it comes to debt repayment and savings, whether you find a financial advisor or simply work with someone at your bank, inexpensive help is available, and motivating. As for understanding tax benefits and programs, a professional accountant could save you their fees many times over.

CHAPTER SIX

Running Your Household

"**S**ARAH CAN'T GO A SINGLE day without spending money, and I can go a week with the same $20 bill in my wallet," Keith will proclaim to guests over dinner. Sure, but can he go a week without using toilet paper, eating groceries or sleeping with blankets and pillows? Does he want to stop sending cards to family members on their birthdays, or bringing a bottle of wine to dinner at a friend's place? It's easy to keep your money in your pocket when you're not the one responsible for keeping groceries in the fridge, gas in the car, clothing on the kids, and every other expense related to running the household.

In this chapter you'll find general information about saving time and money when it comes to running your household, as well as some more specific tips and tricks.

The Cost of Convenience

Whether you have a new baby or five under five, something you'll be perpetually short of is time. One of the hidden costs of having kids is your increased reliance on items of convenience. If you've ever bought a package of toilet paper or a bottle of ketchup from a tiny convenience store out of last-minute desperation, you've probably experienced the sticker shock upon discovering the item is as much as two or three times higher in price than it is at the major supermarket a few kilometres away. It's the price of convenience and, when you're trying to minimize your spending, the cost is often too steep to justify the purchase.

It's easy to see such differences, especially when it comes to food. The ingredients to make five salads are the same price as one prepared salad.

Single serving packages of macaroni and cheese might be four times the cost of preparing the same food from scratch and storing it in reusable containers.

As usual, there are some exceptions to the rule. Sometimes it does make sense to purchase a convenience item rather than making your own from scratch. Pudding cups that used to cost as much as $5 per four pack can now be had for as little as $1 a four pack at the local grocery store. A frozen pizza bought on sale could be half the cost of making it from scratch, and a quarter of the price of ordering in. Whether the quality is the same is debatable.

If the general rule is that convenience costs, why is it that so many businesses don't merely exist but thrive on providing a convenience service? Because in 70% to 90% of Canadian families, both parents work either part- or full-time, and most would prefer to spend the time they do have available for their children on family activities, not vacuuming. Even if one parent is home full-time, the idea that mom or dad has plenty of free time to be lounging on the couch watching soaps is absurd. Many new moms find it difficult enough to change out of their pajamas before dinnertime!

Relying on convenience items allows us to spend more time with our family, get more housework done, and focus on our careers. It frees us from the time-consuming drudgery of scrubbing toilets, or preparing dinner. Yet sometimes we lose out on more than just money by relying on convenience items. Will hiring a house cleaner mean your kids will have fewer chores other than tidying their rooms? Will bringing home takeout rob your children of learning useful cooking skills? You'd be surprised at the kind of bonding that can happen when mother and son chat over a chore like slicing tomatoes. Consider too that convenience can be detrimental to your health. We've all succumbed to the temptation to pick up a fast food meal on the way home from work rather than prepare a meal from scratch. Not only is the $25 it costs to buy the family hamburger meals three times that of preparing a large pot of homemade spaghetti (with leftovers for lunch the next day), the nutritional value of the fast food meal is woefully inadequate and if eaten too often can be detrimental to your health.

When you've added up the many dollars spent on convenience items, could you cut back on work time and incorporate family time into the time spent doing things yourself? If you cancel the cleaning service, stop buying lunches and take-out, and use one less day of daycare, could you work one day less each week? Maybe. What if you move to a smaller house, trade in your cars for older models or smaller, more efficient vehicles, and take cheaper vacations closer to home? Could you cut your work hours to just two days a week? Possibly. More importantly though—do you want to? For some, the answer will be no. And that's OK. Like I said at the outset, this book is not about getting everyone to follow exactly the same plan and end up in the exactly same place, eating noodle cups every night for dinner and forgoing any participation in recreational activites in favour of huge RESP contributions. It's about helping you examine every possibility to find the right financial balance for your family.

Living Space

Is home ownership for you? Contrary to popular belief, home ownership is not in everyone's best financial interest. If housing prices rise you can be sitting on an excellent investment. But to fully realize the potential return on that investment, you have to be willing to sell—and likely buy into the same, higher priced market. There are many significant financial risks to home ownership.

If your budget is stretched to the limit, buying a house, or moving up into a bigger, more expensive home, could cause your budget to snap. Minor setbacks, such as temporary job loss or unforeseen medical expenses, could put your home at risk if you can't meet your monthly payments. Home ownership is more expensive than renting month to month because when the furnace dies, the siding needs repair, or you get a rodent infestation, there's no landlord to call—you're the one paying the bill. Property taxes, home insurance (more expensive than tenant insurance)—you're responsible for all of it.

Is Renting the Right Choice?

Buying your first home is a significant event, and is usually synonymous with entering adulthood. But home ownership is not the perfect financial investment for everyone.

Rent payments are not necessarily throwing away money that would otherwise be building you equity. Equity is the portion of the property that you are building with each mortgage payment (less the interest). As you build equity, the equity is essentially a tax free investment—you are not taxed on the profit from your home when you sell it so long as the home is your primary residence. However, equity takes time to build. It's typical that during your first few years of mortgage payments, you'll be paying mostly interest, and little of the principle amount borrowed.

When housing prices and interest rates are down, you may begin to hear marketing campaigns comparing the benefits of home ownership vs. renting. Initially your mortgage payments might be comparable to rent, but it's important to understand variable interest rates and the many other costs associated with home ownership. An older home will eventually cost additional money for maintenance and repairs, while newer homes usually require many finishing touches, such as sod, fencing, and garages.

Depending on when you buy, there are no guarantees that your house will increase in value. If you believe market prices may fall when you think you'll need to sell your home, either for a new job or another opportunity, you could be stuck losing money on your home investment. There's little flexibility in home ownership when it comes to moving quickly on lucrative relocation opportunities.

One perk of renting is that you won't be tempted to spend money on major renovations—you'll have to make do with what you've got, as most landlords won't allow anything more drastic than a change of paint colour, and while they might cover the cost of the paint, the sweat equity will be in the service of somebody else's asset.

Mortgages 101

So you've decided to buy. Whether you're purchasing a condo, townhouse or single family home, you'll need a mortgage. This is where your budgeting and net worth statement come in handy.

How much is your down payment, and how much will you qualify for? It depends. These numbers are connected to your income, your debt, your credit history, and each other. The larger your down payment, the less you'll need to mortgage. Down payments generally range from 5 to 25% of the purchase price or the appraised value of the property—whichever amount is lower. However, to qualify for a conventional mortgage, you'll need to make a down payment of 20% of the purchase price of the home. If this is your first home, it's unlikely you'll have the funds to make such a large down payment. This will be more likely to occur when you're applying for a mortgage for your second or subsequent home purchases.

Mortgages requiring lower down payments, also known as insured mortgages, are available for both new and existing homes. The monthly expense is higher because your payments include a premium for insurance to cover default of payment.

The amount you qualify for may be much higher than the amount you could actually comfortably pay every month, and still have enough to live on.

If you have a history of steady employment, good credit, and little debt, you'll generally qualify for a mortgage of about three times your family's gross annual income. The amount you have available for a down payment will affect this number as well.

There are two ratios used to calculate the mortgage you qualify for: your gross debt service ratio (GDSR) and your total debt service ratio (TDSR). The GDSR is your monthly mortgage payment plus 1/12th of the annual property taxes, plus monthly utility costs. This figure is divided by your gross monthly income. If the answer to this formula is less than 32%, you qualify. The TDSR is similar to the GDSR except you add the cost of your monthly debt payments to the mortgage payment, property taxes and utility costs. Then you divide this number by your gross monthly income and so long as this number is less than 40%, you qualify under this criterion.

No Money Down Mortgage?

If you don't have a minimum 5% down payment saved, but have still decided to jump into home ownership, you can apply for the Canadian Home Mortgage Corporation's Flex Down package. You can qualify for this program if you have good credit and qualifying income. This program allows prospective homeowners to obtain the 5% down payment from any source, including loans from family members, and cash back incentives offered by banks. Talk to your bank for complete details.

What qualifies as income? If you receive a salary for full-time work, you likely won't have any problems. However, if you work part-time, are on contract, or receive tips, commissions, or bonuses, things become more difficult. You'll need to prove that this income is likely to continue to come into your household. Self-employed individuals must provide two to three years of Notice of Assessments from the federal government.

The amortization period is the total period over which you pay for the mortgage. You can choose an amortization period of up to 35 years. Choosing a shorter amortization period will result in a significant interest savings over the life of the mortgage and equity will build faster. Your monthly payments will be larger.

You can choose between a fixed or variable rate of interest. A fixed rate means the interest rate and payments remain constant to the end of the term. The term is the period during which the interest rate applies, which can be anything from as little as six months to as long as 10 years, depending on the lender. With a variable interest rate, the interest rate fluctuates. While your actual monthly or biweekly payments do not change for the duration of the term, when the rates are lower, more of your payment is applied toward the principle. Usually, you will have the option of locking in for the balance of your term at the current rate of interest if the rates begin to increase.

Always confirm your approval for a mortgage from your banker or mortgage broker before you start your search for a home, and definitely do so before making an offer on any property. In a hot real estate market you could lose your deposit and the house you want if you are unable to confirm your financing approval as quickly as the conditions of sale demand.

A mortgage broker arranges financing for borrowers, either through banks or non-traditional lenders. Mortgage brokers can find better rates than banks may offer. However, they're more likely to be used by families having difficulty getting approval from regular financial institutions, and in these cases, the rates may be much higher.

If you experienced sticker shock at the price of your new home, be prepared for the greater shock after all the associated expenses in buying a home are tallied. The sticker price is just the starting point! The following are additional costs above and beyond the purchase price. While not all of these extras may apply to you, many will, so check with your lender to ensure you'll be able to cover the expenses that do apply to you.

- **Mortgage loan insurance application fee and premium.** If you have a low down payment mortgage, you may require mortgage loan insurance. There is an application fee, and the insurance may be applied to the cost of your mortgage, or you may be required to pay the total amount up front.
- **Home appraisal and home inspection.** If your lender requires a professional home appraisal to determine the estimated value of the home, you're on the hook for the cost, usually between $250 and $350. A home inspection may also be required as a condition of your Offer to Purchase. This is a report on the condition of the home, and usually costs between $200 and $500. Also, be prepared to pay for small repairs recommended by the home inspector if the previous owner refuses to cover the costs.
- **Land registration fees or taxes.** You may owe provincial or municipal taxes or fees upon closing.
- **Property taxes and utilities.** You may have to reimburse the previous homeowner or builder for prepaid property taxes or utilities.
- **Property insurance.** Insurance is required as the home is held as security for the mortgage. Your lender will require a copy of your insurance.

Besides the mandatory costs above, there are a number of other expenses that, while not mandatory, are often very much needed. These include new appliances (if the previous owner has taken them, or they're not in working order), outdoor equipment (lawnmower, hoses), window coverings, moving expenses and utility deposits. There are legal fees to consider and, if you're buying a condo, additional fees are required.

Paying Down Your Mortgage More Quickly

The money saving tips found throughout this book may help your family contribute to RESPs, RRSPs, survive on one income, or just trim your budget and reduce debt. Those unspent dollars could also be used to pay down your mortgage more quickly, reducing your amortization period and the interest you pay over the life of the loan.

Most lenders have a variety of features you can take advantage of without penalty. These may include increasing your monthly payments, making lump sum payments sporadically or annually against the principle, switching from monthly to biweekly payments, or doubling up payments whenever possible. Check with your lending institution and read the fine print.

Our first home was a 1,400 square foot two bedroom bi-level with an unfinished basement. To us, it felt like a mansion. Others warned us that once we had kids, it would be too small. We scoffed at the idea. Families of six would live in houses half this size a few decades ago, we'd reply. The kids can share a bedroom for a few years, we'd assert. Yet soon after Kate was born, that house suddenly seemed so small! Baby equipment sure has a way of taking over all available floor space.

It didn't help that many of our friends were considering moving into larger homes, and this home we were so thrilled with just a few years before seemed cramped and inadequate.

Moving into a larger home in the same community, or a nicer one, can have serious financial implications. If your current house has increased in value, so too has the larger house you're considering buying, and possibly by a greater percentage. If you use a realtor to sell your home, the fees take thousands away from your profit. You'll need to hire a moving van, complete any necessary repairs or improvements to the new home, and furnish the additional rooms. These costs are obviously above and beyond the purchase price of the house.

Can you make do in your current home by spending a bit of money and time to make it more functional and more loved? When Lisa and her husband decided they wanted to move into a bigger, better, and more expensive home, they had an interior designer friend come in to "stage" their present home—to re-purpose and change things in order to show their home in the best possible light. The designer did a great job—so great, in fact, that Lisa decided she no longer wanted to move! So they didn't, and when Lisa decided to open her own business not long afterwards, the extra financial cushion in their day-to-day budget (which would have been eaten up with their new mortgage) allowed her to follow her dream.

Tips To Fall Back in Love With Your Home

Declutter and pare down your belongings to the minimum. Ugly, non-functional furniture should go, boxes from previous moves you've never looked through, toys the kids have grown out of. Why do you have six tablecloths when you only use them on special occasions? Do you really think you'll ever find a use for those old Commodore computer parts? How about those sequined skinny leg jeans for which you never lost the ten pounds required to fit into them?

- **Utilise storage.** Pack away winter or summer items, getting them out of your way for the months they're not needed.
- **Say goodbye to useless things.** Lamps that are never turned on, side tables that hold nothing but impersonal knickknacks, those twenty empty margarine containers—get rid of them all.
- **Look for multi-use furniture.** Consider options like a coffee table with large roll out drawers to hold kids toys, or a bed with drawers underneath for clothing. Storage bins and racks with customised labels will also help maintain order.
- **Utilise wasted space.** Install a shelf above doorways to hold your kids collectibles or for extra towels in the bathroom. Put low shelving or a small dresser in the closet.

- **Roll a new coat of paint on the wall.** Use a colour you've always loved but never dared to try. Take treasured items such as a pin collection out of storage and display them in a unique way. By personalising your home, you'll build a stronger emotional connection to it.

When Kate was a year and a half old, we did decide to move to a larger home. We had arranged a line of credit against the house for my business, and hated having that debt hanging over our heads. So we decided to try to find a bigger house, but one that wasn't quite as nice. We found a 2,400 square foot home in Airdrie, Alberta, where my business was located. Though the neighbourhood was not as new or modern as the one we were selling, we liked it nevertheless, and knew we could do the necessary renovations for a relative pittance. The difference between what we sold our first home for and paid for the new one was significant, and the gain in equity allowed us to reduce our mortgage, relieve the debt load, and finally spread out. In many smaller communities outside the major cities, house prices can be significantly less just a few kilometres away from a pervious address—something to think about.

Rent or Buy

Still not sure which option is best for you right now? Industry Canada's website <www.ic.gc.ca> has a Rent or Buy Calculator. By entering the amount of cash you have available for a down payment, your monthly rent, mortgage rate, expected rate of return on investments, and a variety of other factors, you can determine whether it makes financial sense to buy a home or rent and invest the difference. The calculator assumes that if you rent, you will invest all the money you would have used as a down payment, and that any money saved from renting rather than buying would also be invested.

Moving in with Mom and Dad

It's a growing phenomenon; adult children moving back to the childhood home to live with their parents. Generally, the children choose to move back home because of some unforeseen circumstance or financial hardship. They're called "Boomerang Kids" and, if your parents are in a situation to help you through a brief period, it can be a viable short-term option.

If you're planning on moving in with your parents, be sure to keep the following three points in mind to help make the arrangement as harmonious as possible for as long as is necessary.

- **Determine the why.** Why are you moving back in with your parents? Is it to pay down your debts, or save for a down payment on a house? Is it to transition into a new life situation, such as after a divorce? If possible, set an end date for the arrangement, and be prepared to be questioned regarding your progress towards your stated goal.
- **Outline house rules.** In writing up the ground rules, you will help eliminate many problems and contentious issues before they erupt. Is it assumed that the grandparents be expected to babysit at the drop of a hat simply because they're there?
- **Do your share, and more.** Whether you're paying rent or not, you should still participate in the operation and general maintenance of the household. That means doing chores, running errands, making meals, and buying groceries. Don't be a freeloader!
- **Be sure the house can handle it.** It may not be wise to move in to your parent's home if there's only one television, one common space, etc. Resentment, frustration, and anger can build and permanently damage your relationship if you both have to deal with each others' parenting or grandparenting style in close proximity for too long a period of time.

Must We Get a Minivan?

Are you a two-vehicle family? A lot of married couples don't even consider giving up their second car to save money when kids come along—after all, isn't that when you need it most? How else will you get the kids to doctors' appointments, classes, or other events? In fact, many stay-at-home parents find they get by just fine without a second vehicle—some families appear to manage without any car, even if both parents work. If you live near a good bus route, or within walking distance of things like schools, parks, and grocery stores, having a vehicle could be an unnecessary expense. If a shopping mall is a short car ride away, you're more likely to spend the afternoon there if all you have to load the kids into a car that is always available in the driveway. If you have to do is load the kids into a bus, then navigate home with packages, it's out of the question. What kids want and need most, such as playdates at their classmate's house or a few hours at the park, is often just a short walk away.

Not having a vehicle during the day or not having access to one at all will mean you have to get a little creative with your planning. For the times when they really need a vehicle, the working parent could be driven to and from work by the stay-at-home parent who then has the use of the car for the day. The working parent could join a carpool group one or more days a week, and the stay-at-home parent could find a friend willing to lend a ride occasionally in return for babysitting or a token thank-you gift. You could also look into car sharing groups, popular in big cities where urban dwellers may only need the use of a car for a few hours a month.

If you already have a second (or third) vehicle, do you really know how much it's costing you annually? If you're not tracking your spending on this, you should!

If you're thinking of buying a car and you're contemplating buying brand new, think again. The Canadian Automobile Association (CAA) produces a Driving Costs brochure, and their figures are probably pretty close to your own calculations of the costs associated with car ownership. For 2008, the CAA reports the average commuter spends approximately $8,599 per year for the privilege of driving a newly purchased minivan like a Dodge Grand Caravan. That figure covers insurance, license and registration, finance costs and depreciation. Operating costs such as fuel, maintenance, and tires add another $2,000 per year if you drive just 12,000 kilometres per annum.

There are many reasons people use to justify their purchase of a brand new car. You want a reliable car, right? The money you pay for a new car is money spent more on prestige than safety. A lease-back vehicle a few years old that has been well maintained is no less safe than an overpriced, brand spanking new set of wheels. Speaking of leases, the Industry Canada website <**www.ic.gc.ca**> has a Lease or Buy Calculator you might find helpful if you're considering leasing.

But what about the great prices on new cars? Sure, prices on new cars have dropped, but so has the value of similarly featured used car. If you buy a new car and you have fantastic credit, you may qualify for cash back or low-interest financing. But you will likely also qualify for a very low-interest loan (if you even require financing) for a less expensive used car. This used car may cost more in maintenance and repairs, but you're still going to be ahead of the game. New vehicles lose an average of 20% of their value the instant they are driven off the lot.

Buying a car privately from an individual placing a classified advertisement or from a friend may be the cheapest way to go, but you won't necessarily receive the same security you get when you buy from a big name dealership who will stand behind the purchase. If you're buying from an individual and you're really serious about the car (you've reviewed the paperwork, taken it for a test drive, and like the price) ensure you get a full mechanical inspection performed by a certified mechanic. Don't believe the word of the seller, and don't rely on his mechanic's inspection—get your own. While your mechanic is under the hood, visit a registry with the Vehicle Identification Number (VIN) and ask for a lien search to ensure the car isn't stolen or has money owed on it to a financial institution—if it is, it could be reclaimed by the original owner with no compensation to you.

If you decide to buy from a dealership, do your research. Be prepared with information on the car you're considering buying, and know the street and book values for both private and dealership sales for the same make, model and year in similar condition and odometer readings. When talking prices with any salesperson, don't be the first to state any numbers, such as your price range. If you say you have between $5,000 and $6,000 to spend and you start discussing a $5,000 car, how can you negotiate a lower price with ease? The salesperson already knows you can afford up to $1,000 more. Instead, tell the salesperson about the type of car you want and ask to see similar models. You'll already know for yourself if they're in your price range.

Remember—everything's negotiable. The salesperson expects to negotiate, so be prepared to do that. You've got two basic strategies—offer a sum lower than that which you're willing to pay and negotiate up, or offer exactly what you're willing to pay and don't budge. Personally, I like option number two. Usually the sales agent will leave to speak with a manager. When they come back with a new price, I simply reiterate my original price. After two rounds of bartering, if they haven't come back with the number I want, I leave. These sales tactics are tiring, but nearly everyone uses them or a version thereof. If you shop around, you'll find the same tricks used over and over again to try and get purchasers to buy cars at higher prices. Some sneaky tactics include having another member of the sales team pretend to be interested in the car you're looking at, or telling you someone else is coming back later in the day to make an offer. Always be prepared to walk away. You will find another car.

The salesperson will try to keep you in their office for as long as possible. They know that the more time they can get you to commit to a specific car, the more obligated they know you'll feel to sign the paperwork to seal the deal—even though it's not for the price you want. Even if you've stuck around the lot or showroom for two hours working out a deal, always be prepared to walk away if they don't give you the answer you want to hear. Doing this will show the salesperson how serious you are, and when you return a week later and the car you haggled over earlier is still taking up space on their lot, it'll be yours. Make your new offer $150 less this time, just to make a point!

Shop around for the best insurance rates. While insurance companies, like the banks, are merging and choices are becoming more and more limited, you can still find wildly differing quotes when choosing your automobile insurance. Call a few of the companies listed in the Yellow Pages and get a quote from each.

Ask about group rate discounts. You may be eligible for discounts because of the profession you are in, the company you work for, or university or college you attend or attended. If you don't drive often, ask about low mileage discounts. Do you have a car alarm? It may save you money. If you've never had an insurance claim or ticket, ask for a good driver discount. Graduates of drivers' education programs can get discounts as well.

The key to finding a good service shop that isn't going to rip you off is to ask your family, friends, colleagues, and co-workers for referrals. They'll be able to give you the names of a few places they trust, and you can check them out yourself. I used to take my car to a repair shop that would let me buy used parts from a pick-a-part yard and give it to the mechanic. They would check and install it, and the total cost would be 60% to 70% less than every other price I was quoted.

Do you live in a city with a college or technical school? The automotive repair program might be your ticket to reducing maintenance or repair costs. For a small fee, the cost of parts, or sometimes for no charge at all, students will repair bodywork or mechanical problems. The catch is that what ails your car might not qualify—they may only need automatic vehicles that month, or cars with a certain sort of engine problem. But call anyway—some schools will keep your name on file and will offer to do preventative maintenance. Another downside to this approach to automotive maintenance and repair is they usually need to keep your car a little longer than most other repair shops, and they don't offer services like courtesy cars.

Roadside Assistance

If you're driving an older car, you might want to purchase roadside assistance coverage. It's usually inexpensive—$100 a year or less—and the annual dues can pay for itself with just one incident. Most major roadside assistance plans cover opening your door if you've locked yourself out of your car, a discounted towing service, gas delivery if you run out of gas, battery boosting, and minor emergency repairs. Being a member of a roadside assistance plan may also get you further discounts on insurance or travel.

Making the Most of Meals

Food is the source of one of our greatest expenditures, and one that can spiral out of control faster than you can pick up the phone for delivery. Your spending on food doesn't just include the money you spend at the supermarket—it should include every single food purchase, including your morning caffeine fix, the weekly wing night, and Friday night dinners out.

Have you ever spent $250 at the grocery store only to have the kids whine two days later that there's nothing to eat? Opened the door to the pantry and wondered how it could be crammed full of food, but you can't figure out how to make a decent meal with any of the contents? As a busy and frugal mom, I've found a number of ways to solve the challenge of dinner time in our household.

Soon after the birth of our daughter, my husband and I participated in a taping of the show *Fixing Dinner*, where host Sandi Richard introduced us to her style of meal planning in order to help us minimize the time in the kitchen, and maximize the quality of our meals. We were sceptical at first, but meal planning has become a way of life for us.

How many times have you thrown out a cucumber or tomato that's gone soft in the fridge? What about the half loaf of bread that grew mouldy? Meal planning significantly reduces food wastage. For us, it has also resulted in fewer and less expensive trips to the grocery store, better meals, and more time spent with our children. It can produce the same results in your house too!

Richard has a number of books in her best-selling series Cooking for the Rushed (*The Healthy Family*, *Life's on Fire*, *Getting Ya Through the Summer*, *The Family Dinner Fix*, and *Dinner Survival*). Each book includes quick, easy, and delicious recipes and weekly shopping lists of the items required to make the week's meals. No more wandering the aisles of the store, randomly throwing in whatever looks like it could make a meal. Using Richard's methods, you'll buy only what you truly need. Of the many cookbooks I've collected over the years, I think I've dog-eared more pages in her cookbooks than in all of the others combined!

While you can buy her books and follow the weekly plans as laid out in the books. I've found that my attempts to follow this method too rigidly doesn't mesh with our real life, where dad's eating out for work, I'm off with girlfriends or a work function, or we're having dinner with friends. We'd buy groceries for meals we'd subsequently skip, which defeats the whole purpose. So I follow her concept of meal planning without following the books to the letter.

Meal planning on your own is relatively simple. First, sit down with your family fridge calendar and figure out which nights you need meals for, and start flipping through your cookbooks to find meals you love or want to try. I do this most weekends in conjunction with the sales flyers to find recipes that would best fit the cuts of meat on sale. Be sure to write down which cookbook you grabbed the recipe from, along with the page number. I add a short notation for the next day too—for instance, Thursday might have a recipe title, cookbook title, page number and the note, "take out stewing beef," which reminds me to transfer the meat I'll need for the next evening's dinner from the freezer to fridge before bed.

When you've selected your recipes, do a quick inventory of your pantry and fridge to figure out which ingredients you already have, and write down which ingredients you need to pick up. Each morning I check the recipe for the evening meal to see if I've taken out the required items from the freezer, and often will pull out any pantry items or pots and pans I'll be needing. I leave the cookbook open on the kitchen counter and, if time permits during the day, sometimes I'll tackle a small task like washing and chopping veggies. When it's time to start dinner, it's a quick business, and the meal is healthier, easier, and much cheaper than a last minute call to the pizza place around the corner.

Once a Month Cooking

Personally, I like to cook, and my schedule allows me the 30 to 45 minutes a day to cook with my kids, so daily cooking works most days. But a lot of moms either don't enjoy cooking on a daily basis, or don't have the time or energy. That's where meals made in advance come in handy. Sure, you could stock your freezer with store-bought casseroles, lasagnas and other commercially prepared meals, but the salt and fat content is as outrageously high as the price. What if you could invest just a few hours of time, and have all your cooking done for the month? It's possible! Once a month cooking is a concept that has been around for awhile, but has gained popularity with moms and entrepreneurs alike.

At Once a Month Mom <**www.onceamonthmom.com**> the content author posts a monthly menu complete with 10–15 breakfast recipes, 10 lunch recipes, and 15 dinner recipes with sufficient quantities for two families of four. The menu includes recipes, a grocery list and instructions, plus hundreds of pages of tips, ideas and general discussion on once a month cooking. This is a very detailed website—you could spend hours reading blog updates and long discussions over the best freezing containers, methods and other issues surrounding once a month cooking. It's a great website, and all of the recipes we've tried from it have been winners.

My first night out after Nicole was born wasn't for dinner, a movie, a night with my girlfriends or even a date night with Keith. Instead, I spent the evening at my first Big Cook©. There, along with 17 other women, I spent four hours chopping onions, peeling garlic, mixing, sorting, stirring and washing. Organized by a dietician from the local community, the night was based on a book called *The Big Cook*© <**www.thebigcook.com**>. This cookbook walks you through creating a month's worth of meals with friends—all in one day. The book includes instructions for choosing and using the recipes, creating grocery lists, preparing the meals with friends, and meal storage. You can do a small version, making 8 to 12 meals with one friend, or a huge one with a community group. I went home with 18 healthy meals ready for the slow cooker, the oven or the grill in freezer bags. The cost worked out to just over $13 a meal, all designed to feed 4 to 6 people, perfect for our family. Plus, I had a great time—and with complete strangers! I'm looking forward to organizing more with friends in the future. This can be difficult to do if members of your family have food intolerances or allergies and require a more restrictive or specialized diet as a result.

If you live in a big city, there might be any number of businesses offering once a month cooking events. Finding a community group which plans such events is nearly always a cheaper option.

Shopping Tips

- Use a list and stick to it!
- Individually wrapped foods are more costly in order to cover the price of packaging. It's far cheaper to buy in bulk, and repackage the food in small, reusable containers or snack bags (which can also be rinsed out and reused).
- While the prices are usually pretty good, shopping in bulk or warehouse stores can be dangerous. Though you planned to purchase just a few staples, you may find yourself loading clothes, books, DVDs and more into your car trunk along with your foodstuffs. Try to put only food items in your cart.
- Don't overlook specialty stores for great deals on quality food. Check out bakeries for deals on bread or other baked goods; Oriental supermarkets for great deals on rice, noodles, and other staples; and Italian stores for deals on sauces or pastas.
- Keep a list of the items you most frequently purchase—peanut butter, bread, milk, soup, etc. Keep track of what you pay for each item, so you'll know a good deal when you see it, and won't be suckered into overpaying for something just because the sign said it was on sale.
- You may have cultivated a taste for brand name products, but you don't have a brand name budget. No-name chips, beans, pasta—can you really tell the difference? Taste test a variety of no-name products and see which ones you like and can add to your pantry. You might be surprised at how easy it is to make the switch.
- Use coupons, but use them carefully. Don't buy a product you wouldn't normally buy and may never use just because you have a coupon.
- Some stores post unit prices on their labels, allowing you to easily compare the price of the same product packaged in different quantities. For instance, while the large 2 litre container of tomato juice may seem like the better deal, if the smaller containers have a lower price per ml, you're better off buying several of the smaller containers—so read the shelf labels, or take a calculator along with you.

- Always check your receipt for errors before you leave the store. If you notice a $5 mistake after you've driven all, or even part of the way home, you probably won't return to make the correction.
- If you're just going to wing it rather than plan meals, be sure to shop more often. Many people scrimp at the grocery store, but overcompensate for their empty pantry by eating out more often, thereby blowing their food budget. Shop more often! Buying frozen pizzas for $3.99 each can save you $10 or more over ordering delivery.

Now that you're feeding a family, you should seriously consider purchasing a freezer if you don't already have one. You can usually buy a freezer—new or used—for less than $150 and it'll pay for itself within the year. You don't need anything huge or fancy. Buying perishables in bulk can save you lots of money, and can make food preparation a snap. No more calling for takeout—a frozen packaged pizza is ready in 15 minutes. You can even prepare homemade dough and freeze it for the healthiest option.

Packing a lunch or dinner if you won't be at home can save you hundreds a year. Frozen meals, bought in bulk at a discount food store cost just 99 cents, and cups of soup are even less. Add variety to your packed lunches to ensure you won't want to skip them for an expensive fast food lunch. Leftovers, frozen dinners, canned soup, and sandwiches are all traditional lunch fare, but no one ever said you couldn't have a little fun. Real cheese and crackers, fresh fruit salad, frozen juice boxes, and other unique lunch fare will keep you from buying a lunch out of boredom, and will help keep your child's lunches from going to waste.

Great Recipes at the Click of a Mouse

You don't have to visit a bookstore for expensive, glossy cookbooks to start preparing food at home. Visit <**www.allrecipes.com**> to view thousands of recipes, catalogued by name, type of cuisine, or major ingredient. The website is attractively designed, easy to navigate, and, best of all, it's free. Each recipe has a spot where you can read or post reviews, some of which will have suggestions for easier preparation or ingredient substitutions.

Food—The Anti-Drug

In 2004, the National Center on Addiction and Substance Abuse conducted a Teen Survey and found that teens from families that almost never ate dinner together were 72% likelier than the average teen to use illegal drugs, cigarettes, and alcohol, while those from families that almost always ate dinner together were 31% less likely than the average teen to engage in these same activities. Research by other organizations has shown that teens who frequently eat dinners with their family are less likely than other teens to have sex at young ages, get into fights or be suspended from school, and are at a lower risk for thoughts of suicide. Frequent family dining is also correlated with doing well in school and developing healthy eating habits. This pattern holds true regardless of a teen's gender, family structure, and family socioeconomic standing.

Look for highly rated recipes with plenty of reviews. Another great website is <**www.bigoven.com**>. Big Oven is an interactive website with a variety of search options, including locating recipes using food in season or specific ingredients you already have on hand.

But My Kid is a Picky Eater!

The only good thing about having a picky eater in the house is that usually their tastes run to the inexpensive. Peanut butter on white bread, or plain egg noodles are the kinds of food jags common to young children. Despite having adventurous tastes as babies and toddlers, when they hit the preschool years, the girls suddenly became very selective about what they'd eat. I highly recommend *Picky? Not Me, Mom! A Parents' Guide to Children's Nutrition* by Karla Heintz if you have an issue with picky eaters in your house!

Sleep on It

Saving as much as possible and spending as little as possible are not the same thing. Understanding and living this lifestyle is vital to surviving on less.

Taking a night or two to sleep on a prospective purchasing decision just makes sense. Often you'll find you're better off without the item. An item of clothing on sale for just $35, marked down from $100, isn't a bargain if you'll never wear it. You didn't save $65, you wasted $35. How many of the products gathering dust in your home didn't live up to your initial expectations?

It's time to do a "walk of shame" through your house. Look into your closets, cupboards, drawers, storage space, and bedrooms. Whoops, there's the indoor grill you've used twice. See the juicer you never took out of the box? There, gathering dust, are dozens or hundreds of DVDs you haven't watched since you bought them. How much did you spend on those untouched craft supplies? Oh my—how did the kids get 26 video games, and three gaming systems? Look at all the books you could have borrowed from the library—after all, you've never read them more than once.

If you really want to flog yourself, take a calculator with you on your walk of shame. Keep a running total of the wasted dollars in your closets, on your shelves, and in the pantry. The clothing you never wore, toys that were never played with, duplicates and triplicates of things. How much money would you have saved had you not spent it on all these "I could live without it" things?

Now that you're feeling sufficiently guilty, it's time to purge. I know, you paid good money for those items and you hate to get rid of them and admit that you wasted your money. Cut your losses! Hold a garage sale, sell stuff online, give the items to charity, or ask friends if they want any of the items. Not only might you earn a few dollars, but it's a true lesson in wasteful spending to watch someone walk off with your $89 indoor grill for just $7.

Retailers make lots of money by convincing you to make snap decisions on purchasing an item, especially if it's on sale and there's no easy returns policy. If you're really worried about missing a great deal on something by taking the time to sleep on it, you could also create a "Needs" list for your wallet. Carry it around with you. Pull it out when you're tempted to pull out your credit card. When there's little room in the budget most months for anything but necessities, any time I think about purchasing something, I think about my "Needs" list, and if the item I want isn't on the list, I walk away. The list currently has just one thing on it. A good quality kitchen mandolin slicer for under $40. If I find it, I'll snatch it up. When sweet red bell peppers were overstocked and on sale at our local grocery store for $0.99 for a four pack, I bought ten packs and spent three hours slicing the peppers and filling freezer bags, which are super handy for adding to stir frys. A slicer would have made the job much faster.

Need New-to-You Stuff? Get it for Free

For families on a tight budget, there's no better price than free—especially when in obtaining goods you're doing your part to help the environment. Based on a concept created in 2003, The Freecycle Network™ <**www. freecycle.org**> is a non-profit organization that encourages groups in cities across the world to help the environment and improve their own lives by giving away things they don't need and finding things they do, all without visiting stores or landfills. With nearly two million members in 3,312 communities around the world, there is no end to the things you can find.

Each group is run locally by a volunteer moderator, and membership is free. Greeting cards, baby strollers, weight lifting equipment—you can find pretty much everything and anything, with the exception of alcohol, tobacco, firearms or drugs. Have an old printer gathering dust in your basement? Post an "offered" ad in your city's Freecycle™ group and someone will surely be glad to pick it up. Looking for a dresser for your son's room? Post a "wanted" message, or keep an eye on the offered messages from others. Either way, regardless of whether you have items to offer or are searching for a wanted item—goods are freely given and received.

It's important to note that Freecycle™ is not a place to just go get free stuff for nothing. It's a community—you need to give something in order to receive. For every wanted ad you place you're asked to place a number of offered ads yourself. Think you don't have anything to offer? Impossible! Items offered can be as small as computer cables, old shoes or moving boxes, or as large as vehicles or washer and dryer sets.

Go Green

The past few years have seen a huge increase in interest in "going green". Retailers have been quick to jump on the bandwagon, offering reusable bags, organic clothing, and more. And it's not just about reducing our footprint on the environment. There's often a health and safety issue involved. You have to guard and improve your family's health by buying BPA free baby products, investing in glass food storage containers, buying organic fruits and vegetables, and hormone and antibiotic free meat, etc. On an online forum, a mom posted that she couldn't afford to buy greener products. In fact, truly living "green" is usually about spending less! The main tenets of the green movement are the three Rs—Reduce, Reuse, Recycle. For instance, these days, litter-less lunches are the big thing. So you can buy a special lunchbox for your kids that contains divided containers for $30 or more that is very stylish and funky and totally unnecessary. Instead, a $10 investment in an on sale character lunch box, plus smaller sized reusable BPA free plastic containers will do the same thing. Plus, you'll have a few backups of each mini sized container, and not be on the hook for expensive replacements if your child loses the original containers from the more expensive kit.

In reducing consumption you'll also reduce costs. Do you drink bottled water? Consider buying a jug for your fridge, and filling a travel bottle with water instead. Drink pop by the can? Switch to 2-litre bottles, or water instead. Reuse items until they're absolutely worn out, not just slightly less than perfect anymore.

Here are a few easy ways to reduce your consumption and save money. Some will save you a lot, and otherse will save you just pennies over the years. But combined, they can make a significant difference to your budget. If they interest you, check out the Recommended Reading list below.

- If you pay bills online, keep the return envelope to use for something else (make sure you mark out any addresses or Canada Post lines that look like bar codes).
- Don't waste money on sticky notes when scrap paper will do—save any usable paper with some white space on it for note taking purposes.

Recommended Reading

*If you're interested in finding more ways to save money and reduce consumption, there are thousands of tips available in **The Complete Tightwad Gazette**, available from your local library. Here you'll find tips on how to save money in every facet of life, from food to household repairs to beauty tips. Amy Dacyczyn, the author of **The Complete Tightwad Gazette**, is the frugal guru—there isn't a frugal living tip she misses in her books.*

*While you're at the library, check out **Go Green, Live Rich** by financial expert and best-selling author David Bach. This book outlines fifty ways to make your life, your home, your shopping, and your finances greener—and get rich trying. Look for Kerry K. Taylor's **397 Ways to Save Money** for big picture thinking tips, and Canadian ones to boot, and Pat Foran's **Smart Canadian's Guide to Saving Money**.*

- Create a compost bin in your garden.
- Use less shampoo and detergent when washing your hair, clothing and dishes—it'll still do the job for less money and waste.
- Forgo the expensive cleaners—vinegar and water works just as well for a tenth of the cost.
- Get an online subscription to the newspaper instead of daily delivery.
- Reuse plastic grocery store bags or cloth bags—at some stores each bag will get you a few cents off your bill or earn you customer loyalty reward points.
- Make your own wrapping paper or give gifts in dollar store gift bags—skip the expensive card store wrap. Kids especially love gifts wrapped in the comic pages.
- Forget bagging your lawn clippings—mow the lawn more frequently (with a push mower of course!) and let the clippings enrich the soil.
- Use old Christmas cards as Christmas tags by simply cutting out the design on the card.

- Use plastic milk jugs or ice cream buckets filled with water in the freezer to fill empty air space, thereby reducing the cost of cooling after openings.
- Practice "precycling"—buy products that use the least amount of packaging or contain recycled materials.

Utilities

Utilities have the surprising power to consume a lot of cash flow each month. From electricity and gas, to sewer, cable, and phone service, here are several ways that you can cut your utility costs.

General Tips

- Keep the heat at the lowest temperature you're comfortable with, and turn it down when you're sleeping or not home. Grab a sweater instead of turning up the thermostat.
- Limit the use of air conditioning, and consider using a portable air conditioner or room air conditioner rather than cooling the entire house. Often only one or two rooms require cooling.
- Buy energy wise appliances. If you're buying new appliances, choose ones that are energy efficient.
- Turn out lights when you leave a room for long periods of time, and switch to more energy efficient light bulbs.
- During the winter, keep your south-facing windows uncovered during the day to allow the sunlight to enter and cover all windows at night to reduce the chill from cold windows.
- During the summer, keep the window coverings closed during the day to prevent solar gain. Consider installing exterior blinds—solar gain is best prevented by reducing heat before it travels through the glass.
- Install low-flow faucets and showerheads.
- Take more showers than baths and take shorter showers instead of longer ones.
- Be sure your dishwasher is full, but not overloaded, when you run it.

- Let your dishes air dry by turning off the dishwasher after the rinse cycle and propping open the door.
- Turn the stovetop burners or oven off several minutes before the cooking time is finished. The heating element or oven will stay hot long enough to finish the cooking without using more gas or electricity.
- Use appliances like toaster ovens, crock pots or microwaves for small meals rather than your large stove or oven.
- Wash your clothes in cold water using cold-water detergents.
- Wash and dry full loads.
- Clean the lint filter in the dryer after every load.
- Try air-drying clothes on clotheslines or racks.

EnerGuide for Houses Grant

The Government of Canada offers a program designed to encourage those with older homes to receive grant money of up to $5,000 as an incentive for retrofitting their homes to make them more energy efficient.

To qualify, homeowners must have a professional conduct an EnerGuide for Houses evaluation to receive their initial EnerGuide for Houses rating. This energy audit will provide recommendations for improvement. Once some or all of the recommendations are implemented, another audit is conducted, and a new rating is assigned to the home. The amount of the grant depends on the difference between the pre and post ratings. For example, a house with an initial rating of 62 may increase to a rating of 73. This would result in a grant of approximately $750. Depending on the costs involved in making the upgrades, the grant money, along with the annual savings in utilities, could cover the cost of the upgrading. See <www.energuideforhouses.gc.ca/grant> for details.

An EnerGuide for Houses evaluation can cost up to $350. Get a few price quotes before you book the evaluation, as some companies receive subsidies from the Government of Canada and their prices will reflect this. Finally, don't take too long to make the upgrades, as your advisor must submit the application, including the follow-up evaluation, within 18 months of your initial evaluation.

Telephone

Though the price of long-distance telephone service has gone down in recent years, the price of residential service has risen. You may have a choice when it comes to your home phone provider or you may have just one company you can use. You could also use just a cell phone if you don't make a lot of calls, or if you have a comprehensive cell phone plan.

If you make a lot of long distance calls, review the prices on calling plans. Some plans offer the same rate all day, or have unlimited calling for a set fee. Also check to ensure you're making use of the additional features you're paying for. I was amazed to discover I had been paying $7 a month for caller ID—a feature my phone wasn't even capable of providing!

Need a cell phone? Some people are opting to get rid of their home phones entirely, and merging their home and cell phones into one. Research the different packages available, and try not to be swayed by a bells and whistles phone if it comes with a massive contract. When I downgraded from my email and web browsing-capable cell phone to a basic model, I cut my bill by two thirds, and freed myself from being shackled to work. Finally, check with your home insurance company— there may be implications to your rate for not having a land line in the home.

Entertainment

Even if something's free, there are usually plenty of opportunities to spend your money while enjoying a free event. Because it should be all about having fun rather than not spending money, try these tips to avoid pulling out your wallet.

- Eat before you go and bring water and snacks—don't leave the house hungry or you'll spend mucha moola on a fast food fiasco.
- Leave your wallet at home. If you only take a few bucks for bus fare, you won't have to worry about temptation getting the best of you.

- Take poor friends! If your friends are financially strapped too, they won't pressure you to spend more than you should.
- Libraries contain a wealth of fun stuff. From novels to CDs to cookbooks and magazines, your local library has it all. Many libraries now allow you to search catalogues, reserve, and renew books online. You can also take out copies of magazines, or sit and read current issues. Register your kids for the reading programs— they'll have fun learning, and can win prizes too!
- Your local library should also have a great program of interactive seminars and classes. Learn how to start a container garden, write a resume, learn a new language or build a website. There are also great educational classes for kids in addition to the ever popular story time session.
- Add stimulation and variety to your life by volunteering. You'll get to do something fun, get warm fuzzies, and set a good example for your children. You can volunteer for local events, concerts, or charities, and your local free weekly paper or community newsletter may have listings of agencies looking for volunteers. Children's theatres and children's festivals may offer fun volunteering opportunities for the whole family.
- Spend your Saturday at the flea market—snack on free samples while touring relics from your parent's era. Let the kids hunt for the best deal a loonie will buy.
- How long has it been since you've had homemade cookies? Spend a day baking proper cookies, or make a cake from scratch or a pre-packaged mix, and let the kids go wild with the decorating.
- Check the free weekly newspaper listings for inexpensive or free events scheduled in your community.
- Chances are one of your children has accumulated a ton of books and movies. Make their collection available to friends in return for access to their collections, and everyone will get to enjoy something new for free!
- Sign up for the online newsletter produced by your local video store. You'll sometimes get coupons for free or discounted rentals, and can enter fun contests to win cool movie stuff.

- Buy an inexpensive kite and spend the day at a park.
- Pick up an astronomy book from the library and head out of the city to enjoy stargazing. Make it a summer treat the kids can look forward to year after year.
- Dust off your bicycles and go out for a ride with the kids. Pull out your ice skates, pour hot chocolate into a thermos, and go skating at an outdoor rink.
- Coupons are a lifesaver! You'll find coupons for most every attraction in your city, as well as deals on restaurants, services, and even grocery stores. Keep ones you may use on the fly in your wallet for quick access. Look for coupons or free offers everywhere—in junk mail flyers, newspapers left out on a desk, and even your phone bill may come with coupons. You can also find coupons online at <**www.save.ca**> or <**www.coupons.com**>.
- Need time for yourself? Instead of a girl's night out at the bar, host a sleepover for mommies. Pop popcorn, watch a chick flick, and reconnect with your girlfriends.
- Visit a local park and roast weenies and marshmallows in the fire pits.
- Some museums have a free admission day—pack a lunch and avoid the gift shop.
- Do a little exploring in a small town nearby your big city centre. Check out the stores, tourist spots, and local atmosphere.
- Pack a picnic and visit a local lake, or take a drive in the country. Bring a blanket and your camera.
- Think like a tourist—go for a stroll in your city's shopping districts, window shopping only. Visit the historic spots you've only driven by.
- Cable television service is a good example of an expense you can reduce. Not only will you likely watch less television and have more time to pursue interests as individuals and as a family, but you'll also save some money. If it's too difficult to think about giving up cable then just give up a premium channel or two. Another tip: for Internet access dial-up isn't chic, but it's cheap. If you don't use

the Internet much, or only for email, see if dial-up is sufficient for your needs.

Staying Healthy

Eating properly and taking care of your body are the two best ways to stay healthy and avoid costly trips to the dentist, chiropractor, or other health care provider. Eating healthy home-cooked meals is always cheaper than eating fast food and processed meals, and exercising (beyond a pair of walking or running footwear) doesn't have to cost a penny. Yet you still might be throwing away thousands a year on diet programs, books or pills, and gym memberships or equipment. Here are some ways to save on common health care costs:

- Practice good oral health—brush and floss regularly, and go to regular cleanings and checkups. Money spent on preventive care is money well spent.
- Check your local dental schools to see if they need volunteers for procedures like cleanings and fillings. While in university, I signed up to be a filling volunteer and received an all expenses paid trip to Halifax (where I was able to squeeze in two days of visiting family) in exchange for letting a dental student do their filling test on me at the university dental school.
- Check your community health services centre to see if reduced-fee dental care is available for families in financial need.
- When it comes to eye exam costs, shop around. Being aware of sales at various optical stores could mean getting a higher quality pair of glasses for the same price as a lower quality pair at a discount store.

Fitness Ideas That Won't Break the Bank

You don't have to belong to a gym to become or remain physically fit. There are lots of great ways to get fit that don't require an expensive gym memberships. Here are just a few ideas, courtesy of Joan Bell, mom of two and the owner of *The Airdrie Yoga Studio*:

- Resistance training: Use your own body weight to get in shape. Push ups, crunches, lunges, squats, bridge pose, and stair climbing/hiking can all be done at home or outside in the backyard or local park on a sunny day.
- Invest a little money in a good resistance band, weighted ball, and hand weights and check out the Internet for a wide variety of exercises you can do from home.
- Rent or purchase a fitness DVD. Big box stores carry reasonably priced fitness videos from aerobics to yoga. Check your local library for fitness DVDs, books, or videos. Don't like to work out alone? Invite a friend to come over in the morning for a workout and coffee.
- Take the dog and go for a brisk walk. Put the little ones in the stroller and do some window shopping. It doesn't have to be intense to count as exercise.
- Wear a pedometer to count your steps. Aim for at least 10,000 steps daily to maintain good health.
- Plan an exercise date with your partner. Go biking or walk around the neighbourhood. Get out your yoga mats and follow a couples yoga DVD.
- If you find exercise boring, then combine your workout with other tasks like reading a book while you ride a stationary bike (check the newspapers for cheap or free exercise bikes) or doing crunches while watching television (instead of going to the fridge for something to eat)!
- Plan a picnic with friends and include some fun physical activities—three legged races, egg tosses, sack races—all the fun activities from your childhood. Have ribbons for the winners!
- Go geocaching and hunt for hidden treasure. This great pastime includes walking, hiking, and searching out clues using a GPS. Visit <**www.geocaching.com**> to check out hunts in your area.
- Join the kids on the trampoline, in a game of tag or fox and goose in the snow. Go tobogganing, for a ride in a swing, or climb on the jungle gym. Kids have the right idea—it is not exercise, it is play.

- Train for a race or join a local running group. Most cities have free or reasonably priced running groups.
- Go dancing with your partner or just shake it up at home. Turn on the tunes and let loose. Or try a new type of class and learn the moves to rhumba, cha cha, salsa and more.
- Jump for joy! Buy a skipping rope at the dollar store and try this great way to work out. Remember hula hoops? Now they have heavier hoops intended for adults. This is a great way to work on your abdominal muscles.
- Instead of going out for dinner and a movie on date night, go bowling, miniature golfing, swimming, or dancing. Just keep moving!

Cleaning

I think I'm in the majority when I state that I strongly dislike house cleaning. I love having a clean house, but I hate being the one who actually has to do the cleaning. So over the years, we've tried various ways of dividing up the responsibilities for keeping our house orderly, including hiring house cleaners to handle it for us. While I love having someone else clean my house, looking at the expense on an annual basis ($100 every two weeks is $2,600 a year) I can't get over the cost, and find myself swishing that mop around and grumbling to myself.

I've found the easiest way to keep a house clean enough to maintain contentment is to enlist help and enforce it. A two-year-old can pick up her toys when she's done playing with them. She can stack her books on the shelf, and line her shoes up by the door. A four-year-old can load the dishwasher. A six-year-old can vacuum. Chores are part of what every member of the household does as part of their responsibility for living in that household. They're not put off or left half done. Everyone pitching in is part of the way we do things, just as being respectful to each other, going to bed at a certain time, and eating healthy foods are part of what we do in our family.

Try to make cleaning easier—instead of having newspapers left on the table to pile up, place a decorative basket in one corner of the kitchen designed to hold them until recycling day. Deal with mail as it comes in, putting bills next to the computer, junk mail in the recycling basket, etc. Got a two-story house? Keep a basket at the top and bottom of the stairs to toss things in that need to be on the other floor, and carry it with you for proper sorting the next time you go up or down.

We've also had to be willing to let our standards slide from where they were before we had kids. Vacuum everyday? Not in our house. Once a week is just fine for us. Laundry often reaches the "oh no we're all out of socks" stage before I dedicate a day to switching loads and sorting and hanging. On an online bulletin board I frequent, one mom posted the following question: Is your home company-ready? That is, would you be happy with how clean your house was if company, or your mother-in-law popped over unannounced? Most answered no, but my answer was yes, absolutely. We'd simply kick our way through the shoes at the door, move the cookbooks off the kitchen table chairs, wash a few mugs and enjoy a good coffee and better conversation. You won't look back at your life and think about the hours spent cleaning your sinks—you'll remember the times spent with loved ones instead.

Bank on It

Do you still have the same bank account your parents helped you open when you were 12, or do you switch companies every year, and have more credit cards in your wallet than family photos? Though few of the big banks offer free banking anymore, many non-traditional banks such as ING Direct™ and President's Choice Financial® (PC Financial) offer free banking, credit cards with no annual fee, and higher interest savings accounts. Are you taking advantage of the best your bank has to offer? Are you with the best institution overall?

Call around to find the best deal and, if they don't offer it, but you like the bank's location or hours, ask for the deal anyway, letting them know who does offer that option. Don't choose a bank that has no bank machines, or branches you can't get to easily. You may get a million free services when you do manage to find their machine, but if you have to pay a $2 service charge every time you withdraw cash from another bank's machine, the extra fees can add up quickly.

Ask to have some services thrown in at no charge—the worst they can say is no. Just by asking I frequently received free overdraft protection, a valuable feature for months where my bank balance hovers near the $5 mark. Don't rely on your overdraft though—it's not free cash, it's a high interest loan. There's little worse than depositing a pay cheque only to find it barely brings your balance up above zero, the rest having been sucked up by your overdraft. It's a deep hole to dig out of.

Keep a close eye on the extra fees. You may be paying steep fees for not having a certain amount of money in your account, or even fees for paying your credit card balance off in full!

Choosing the right bank can make your budgeting even easier. With banks that offer free banking, such as President's Choice Financial® or ING Direct™, you can set up multiple accounts for car repair, gifts, vacation spending, etc., at no charge. You can then set up automatic withdrawals from those accounts accordingly.

The Plastic

Speaking of banking, how many credit cards do you have? What is the limit on each card? The interest rate? The balance? How much are you paying in fees and interest each year? Are you collecting points or other rewards on your card? Is your reward program a valuable one?

If you don't know the answer to the questions above, it's a very bad sign. A high interest rewards card may earn you $200 a year in rewards, but if you're carrying a significant balance, switching to a low interest card with no rewards program could save you over a thousand dollars a year, or more. Have you been tempted by the low introductory rates offered by some credit card companies? Read the fine print: your transferred balance may have the lower interest rate, but if you keep spending on the card, the payments you make usually go towards the transferred balance first. So the low interest amount could be paid off over a few months while the high interest new purchases sit there costing you big bucks.

Carrying balances on your credit cards is possibly the worst kind of debt to have, and if you're doing it on a regular basis, it's time to see a financial advisor or even just your banker to talk about a consolidation loan. They'll advise you to cut up your credit cards in order to ensure you don't just rack it right back up again—important advice to follow.

Get Outta Town

The kind of low-cost travelling on a budget of $20 a day you took before having children generally isn't the kind of trip you'll enjoy quite as much once you have to lug around car seats, strollers, baby formula and a jumbo pack of diapers. Instead, you'll probably be interested in places that have facilities and activities just for children and, unless you want to pull them out of school for a few days, you may have limited windows of time in which you can leave town.

Your idea of what vacations cost will likely have a lot to do with how you vacationed as a child. There were no trips to California theme parks in my childhood; summers were spent in a rundown cabin where the menu was limited to hot dogs and generic brand potato chips. Of course, I thought it was heaven. It was only after becoming an adult that I realized many families assume their annual vacation will cost as much as a used car. As Canadians, nationwide, we're blessed with amazing landscapes and areas perfect for fun family camping trips. There simply aren't any hotels available for the $25 a night for a family of four, which is what a fantastic camping site next to a park and beach will run you. A $500 investment in camping gear—bought either used or in end of season sales—will ensure you have years of great memories for hundreds of dollars instead of thousands of dollars.

Tips for More Affordable Vacations

Have a family meeting to hear about everyone's dream vacation—you might find the kids have been pining for a family camping trip instead of the week long resort extravaganza you had originally planned or thought they wanted.

Consider travelling on the shoulder of a season and/or taking the kids out of school for a few days—travelling for a week in high season on school break is a sure way to spend hundreds or thousands more at the same resort or hotel.

Sell-offs are a great way to get a hard-to-beat deal on a trip somewhere, but you have to be ready to go at the drop of a hat. Before kids, we'd book a week off work but not the trip—then two to three weeks before our week off, we'd book the trip on a sell-off website at a significantly reduced cost. You may not get the exact resort you wanted, but the savings are considerable, and can make any compromise more than worthwhile.

If you collect rewards program points, see if you can cash them in for a vacation or part of a vacation. You may also get a discount on services such as car rentals just for being a cardholder. For the most flexibility, see if you can redeem your miles for gift cards to a travel agency that offers sell off vacation packages—you have near total flexibility if they honour the gift cards as if they were cash.

While on the road, whenever possible, buy your food from local grocery stores instead of restaurants. Stock up on muffins, juices boxes, and bottled water. Your food budget will add up quickly if you're buying overpriced bottled water and unhealthy single serving snacks.

Think about vacationing with friends or family. A rented condo or vacation home means splitting the accommodation cost and, with your children's friends in tow, you'll spend less on structured entertainment. You can take turns making meals around fun themes instead of eating out.

Money Smart Mom Tip

*"We stay in places with kitchens rather than conventional hotel rooms. Vacation Rentals by Owner <**www.vrob.org**> is a great website for finding places that fit the bill."*

Risa, mom of two

Final Thought

We'd all be a lot better off if we stopped comparing ourselves to the Jones's, but it's hard when you can hear them in their hot tub over the sound of your basic cable package. Striving for bigger and better when it comes to material things like houses, vehicles, furniture, and more is a no-win game. It's far more productive to spend your time appreciating what you do have and making it last than chasing after the latest and greatest.

CHAPTER SEVEN

Maxing Out the Credit Cards

I F BABY IS ON THE WAY, one of the worst things you can do is start hitting baby department stores with your credit card in hand. It's time to do some rethinking about what you need, what you want to pay, and making your purchases without going into debt.

New versus Used

It is so easy to prepare for your new baby by simply parking at the nearest baby store and loading your cart with everything the store clerk tells you you'll need. But when parents tell you to cherish every moment because "they grow so fast," remember that this speedy development also means they grow out of things equally as fast! The sleeper that fit the first month of life is probably going to be too tight by the sixth week, and the rattles that baby was so attached to will be gathering dust by the fourth month. While I recommend buying a new car seat, pretty much everything else you need can be quite easily obtained used but still in excellent condition.

Friends of ours were always buying the very best new toys for their baby, and we were definitely envious. Their baby had the best of the best—the $1200 convertible toddler bed, the $75 car seat toy. We were impressed that they could afford all these things, when we definitely couldn't. One day, I asked the mom how hard it had been to get the Alberta government's Centennial $500 RESP grant, and she admitted that they hadn't applied for it yet—they didn't have the money to invest in RESPs. I was floored. Can you picture that conversation 18 years from now? "Sorry honey, we didn't save for your education. But man, you should have seen the exersaucer you had when you were six-months-old!"

The encounter reminded me that in this day and age, it's easy to appear to have more money than you really do. The bank is willing to give you a huge mortgage, the credit card companies are more than happy to increase your limit at every turn, and even toy and baby clothing stores now offer credit cards! You don't have to have money, you just need to have enough money to pay the minimum on your debt load.

In the summer of 2005 a *Calgary Herald* article entitled "Posh Babies" shared interviews with parents who were spending thousands of dollars a year to outfit their baby in Baby Burberry and other designer clothes. The article quoted Dalan Bronson of retail analyst J.C. Williams as saying, "People are prepared to spend money where they see value, and they're not prepared to take risks, especially when it comes to their children." Exactly what risks am I taking by *not* spending $400 on a diaper bag, or by choosing a $4 baby blanket over one costing $94? The only thing I'm risking is my reputation with the Jones's. And frankly, they won't be around to pay tuition for my three girls.

One concern many new parents have about buying used items is that they might be investing in something that could harm their child. Many experts recommend not buying specific items used, such as cribs or car seats, because of unseen or invisible damage. When purchasing a used car seat, ensure to do so from a friend, family member, or a colleague— someone you trust who can tell you the seat has been properly maintained, cared for, and has never been in an accident.

Consignment Stores

If you've never shopped in a consignment store, or just haven't visited one recently, you're in for a real treat. Today, many children's consignment stores have transformed themselves into upscale boutique environments. In addition to offering great clothes at less than half the cost of traditional new retail, they usually stock accessories and baby gear, even cribs and strollers, depending on the size of the store. Many stores also carry new specialty products that are difficult to find or that you wouldn't want to buy used, such as swim diapers, crawling pants, or gift items if you're shopping for someone else. Because consignment store staff only accept what will sell and what they can get a good price for, the items found at consignment stores are typically in excellent condition. Store owners simply won't accept clothing that is stained, ripped, missing buttons or snaps, shows excessive wear or is out of fashion, and baby toys and other equipment must also be in pristine condition.

Shopping at a consignment store doesn't just mean you can get a better price than buying new, it can also often mean that your dollars will get a better quality product than you would have if you had bought new. For instance, the cheapest playpen I found new was $60, and it was as basic as they come. In contrast, at a consignment store, I found a playpen for $50 that included a detachable bassinet, with a sunshade and a mobile. New, this particular playpen was $150.

Thrift Stores

If you frequent a few nice consignment stores, you'll quickly notice a big difference in quality between the products they stock as compared with the typical thrift store. Thrift stores usually don't quite measure up. Thrift stores are often poorly lit, badly organized, and full of junk. There are always hidden treasures to be found in thrift stores if you can take the time to look. Thrift stores also typically charge less for their merchandise than do consignment stores. Expect to pay $1.99 or less for a newborn item of clothing, $2.99 or less for a toddler, $1 for a small toy, $3.99 for a larger toy, etc.

Classifieds

When you're living frugally, the classifieds are also a great way to find larger items such as cribs, swings, change tables, and toddler beds.

Garage Sales

Most frugal parents are well versed in the art of garage sale shopping. Remember that playpen with all the bells and whistles? At a garage sale, I found the exact same model for even less than it was being sold at the consignment store—just $20.

Money Smart Mom Tip

"I usually shopped solely at consignment stores for my son's clothing, but one day I stopped at the thrift store on a whim. I found a toy which sold new for $19.99, and it was available for just 69 cents! All I had to do was cut off the teething ring—which was badly chewed—and throw the toy in the wash. It looked brand new, and it became one of his favourite toys. It's often worth checking out the thrift stores."

Cherie, mom of two

I've lost count of the number of times I've seen items still available at a garage sale at 4:00 pm on a Sunday priced for less than what I could get for them in my store, and they're still sitting there with no buyers in sight. The yard sale operator would probably have made more money and dealt with less hassle if they had first brought these items to a consignment store. I'm often asked why there might be no demand for items, even at fire sale prices and conversely, a consignment store may have waiting list even when the items are more expensive. There are a couple of reasons. Firstly, shopping garage sales isn't consistent—you could spend a tank of gas and a whole morning driving around looking at chintzy vases and boxes of mouldy cassette tapes with narry a baby swing in sight. Secondly, even a seasoned garage sale shopper like me sometimes wastes money buying items that aren't what they promised to be once brought home. Finally, there are no return policies at garage sales—it's buyer beware.

Here are a few tips for more effective garage sale shopping:

- Go out every weekend. Every Saturday morning I'd spend the first two hours of the morning at garage sales.
- The early bird gets the worm. If a sign says the sale runs Friday, Saturday and Sunday, go on Friday. The best stuff always goes first.
- Look for signs that specifically mention baby gear, or multi-family sales.

- Check out sales in neighbourhoods with many new families.
- Bargain! The people running the garage sale expect to sell the item for less than the marked price. Buying $25 worth of stuff? Offer them $18 for the lot, and you'll get it for $20.
- Carry small bills for better bargaining. It's embarrassing to offer $16 for $20 worth of stuff and then pay with a $20!
- Bring your own screwdriver and batteries. Keep a container in your car with at least six batteries of AA, AAA, D, and C for testing any items that require batteries. A classic garage sale selling tactic is to tell a buyer the item works, but they took the batteries out to sell it, when they know very well the battery compartment is damaged by corrosion and there's no chance of the item ever working again.
- Bring your own bags or a cardboard box or two—sellers often forget to have these handy.
- If you're considering an item, pick it up while you continue to shop or think about the purchase. You may turn around for it and it's in someone else's paws.
- Take a friend for company (and a second opinion)!

If you don't have the time or inclination to shop at garage sales, check with the community centres. Often they'll have an annual or spring and fall kids' stuff sale, which is essentially one huge garage sale.

Equipping the Little One
The prices in the following table (see p. 126) are actual prices found in the summer of 2009 while comparison shopping.

Baby Shower Bonanza

One of the most amazing things about having a baby is the sheer volume of gifts people will buy for you. Family, friends, co-workers, and even friends of those people will shower you with gifts. I received a handmade quilt for my first daughter given to me by a woman I've never met!

Comparative Price Ranges of Major Baby Equipment

Item	New	Consignment	Garage Sale
Crib	$100–300	$75–125	$20
Crib Mattress	$45–115	$30–75	$10
Bedding[1]	$50–150	$10–45	$5
Large Stroller	$125–400	$75–200	$45
Exersaucer	$50–150	$30–60	$10
Playpen	$75–250	$75–125	$25
Baby Swing	$50–200	$50–100	$15
Vibrating Chair	$20[2]–75	$20–50	$10
Floor Activity Centre	$40–80	$20–50	$5
High Chair	$40–200	$40–80	$10
Baby Monitor	$20–150	$15–75	$5
Sleepers (3 month size)	$10–25	$7–10	$2

[1] inclusive of sheets, blanket, and bumper pad.

[2] in a half off sale, regulary $40.00

Baby showers are traditionally held only for the first child as a way to help defray the initial costs of having a baby. Too often though, a mom-to-be will find she's received ten six-month sleepers (when three will do), seasonal outfits that won't fit the child when the right season rolls around, a dozen collectible figurines, or a load of 7 lb baby outfits when she's delivered a 10 \lb plus darling. Instead of dealing with the hassle of returning the unsuitable items, or worse, being caught re-gifting them, why not offer your guests some direction? Done tactfully, those attending the shower will appreciate knowing they've either given or contributed towards something you really need.

Work with the person hosting the party to select a theme for the event of gift-giving, and include it on the invitations. If guests ask, be sure to let them know that they don't have to stick to the theme if they have another gift in mind. After all, it's their money, and you don't want to appear as if the only thing that matters is the gift! Cherie's friends threw her a shower where the theme was billed as "Books & Bottoms". Guests brought a bag of diapers and a book they loved as a child, or one their own child favoured. You can specify which brand of diapers you'll be using, or let them choose—you can return them for store credit at most places. You could also request a "Feeding Family" theme—everyone brings a homemade meal ready for the freezer (with the recipe and reheating instructions on a card) to save mom's sanity after baby arrives. Having twins? Ask the shower host to have a "Noah's Ark" theme where everyone brings two of something!

Money Smart Mom Tip

"Unfortunately not every expectant mother is fortunate enough to have a baby shower. For a variety of reasons, I was one of them. In buying items that were on sale, we were able to purchase everything we needed except the crib for ourselves. I was surprised to discover that I took pride in providing for my baby rather than having everything given to us. However, there are still times when I silently sulk about the pregnancy milestone I missed."

Natalie, mom of two

When you're invited to a baby shower, consider choosing one gift that can be your special signature gift. This will make the item memorable. Ensure you stay within your budget. If it's someone I don't know very well, or with whom I'm not particularly close, I buy the year's baby coin collection from the Canadian Mint. It's a gift in my price range, and it's a very special keepsake. For close friends, I make extra large receiving blankets (ideal for swaddling, when normal receiving blankets just don't cut it) out of soft flannel, but they're a bit pricier and more time consuming.

Money Smart Mom Tip

"My second shower was three weeks after my son was born, and everyone who came to the event was asked by the hostess to bring a frozen dish for me and my family, as well as a small gift. I left with two giant coolers full of frozen entrees and baking. It was really nice to have good meals during those first few weeks of sleepless nights and breastfeeding!"

Jen, mom of three

Baby Shower Etiquette

- Traditionally, baby showers used to be hosted by a non-relative, but this has gone the way of the dinosaur. These days, it appears that anyone can host a baby shower, especially close loved ones, like mothers and sisters. Etiquette still dictates, however, that you should not host a shower on your own behalf.
- Showers are normally held a month or two before baby arrives, but some people consider this bad luck, and prefer to hold the shower after the baby is born. It's up to you and your hostess to decide.
- Many people hold showers only for the first baby, but this is another rule that's changing with the times. It's not uncommon to have a shower for the second child, especially if the second child is a different gender than the first.
- Cash is not a theme! Though there are some cultures where asking for cash is perfectly acceptable, Canadian culture dictates that asking for cash is a bit crass. It robs much of the fun of the event and can make you look greedy. However, if people ask what you really want, feel free to say that you're saving up for a specific item, so cash would be wonderful, but of course, anything the individual selects would be similarly appreciated.
- Be sure to send personal thank-you cards for every gift you receive, and thank the hostess with a small gift as a token of your appreciation.

Beg and Borrow

Try to borrow from friends those big ticket items you would like to own for the purposes of a test-drive. If your find they work well for you, you can buy them if you need to give the loaner back before your baby has outgrown their need for the item. I borrowed many things at first, intending to replace them when I found inexpensive new versions. Luckily Kate grew out of needing them before I had to return them, and I never did purchase many items.

Finding First-Rate Freebies

Sign up for an anonymous email account before you begin signing up for freebies. Though most websites claim to protect your privacy and not sell your email address to spammers, somehow your inbox will inevitably fill up with garbage, and you don't want that coming into your regular email account!

Online Freebies

- <**www.pampers.com**> Sign up to receive newsletters, coupons, and free product samples, and enter contests to win Pampers supplies.
- <**www.huggies.com**> Sign up to receive newsletters, coupons, and free product samples, and enter contests to win Huggies supplies.
- <**www.enfamil.ca**> Join Enfamil First Connections to receive a free sample of Enfamil A+, coupons, and a keepsake box to track your baby's growth and development.
- <**similac.ca/en/similac-welcome-addition-addition-club**> Join the Similac Advance Welcome Addition Club to receive product samples, coupons, a magazine and sometimes a free gift, such as a baby bottle bag.
- <**www.nestle.ca**> Joining the Nestle Baby Program and receive a free subscription to their magazine, free samples, coupons, and more.
- <**www.save.ca**> Save.ca is a free service providing coupons online. Just choose your province of residence, select the coupons you

want, and the coupons will be mailed to you the very next day, for free!

- <**smartcanucks.ca**> This is a huge online community where members can find deals, discounts, coupons, freebies, contests and more.

- <**www.welcomewagon.ca**> Welcome Wagon hosts are usually women who deliver a basket or box of gifts, coupons, brochures, and more. Visits are short, free, and available upon request. You can expect to receive free copies of parenting magazines, coupons for diapers, formula, and other baby products, samples of products, and literature from local service providers, daycares, baby groups and more. You may subsequently receive a lot of calls from the businesses included in the basket though, as they receive your phone number in exchange for the gift they gave to you.

Baby Fairs

Many health regions hold prenatal baby care events, or fairs, that are free for expectant and new parents. Participants learn about breastfeeding, sleep patterns, safety, community resources and more. Expectant mothers usually receive a free gift and can enter contests to win prizes.

Money Smart Mom Tip

"Coupons, coupons, coupons! I joined every club out there. I went trigger happy on the internet for diaper clubs, formula clubs, and baby activity clubs. I even signed up my brother so I could get doubles! Similac and Good Start sent me formula, monthly coupons and even Baby Stages  *magazines with helpful advice. Good Start was just as cheap with the coupons as the cheapest alternative brands of formula, and they even sent me coupons for a free can of formula. I loved it! Similac gave me a baby bottle bag and free formula. Pampers and Huggies sent monthly coupons and samples of product."*

Amber, mom of two

How We Shop

In 2001, a University of Alberta business professor conducted a study to see how the presence of strangers at the time of purchase would affect our buying decisions. Jennifer Argo sent 200 people into a store with $5 and instructions to buy batteries. The participants did not have to tell Argo which brand of battery they purchased, and were told they would be able to keep the change. The three batteries offered for sale were a brand name package at $4.29, a $3.69 generic brand, or a mid-range pack priced at $3.99. Argo then sent one or three people into the store to stand nearby while the consumer made their purchase. When the shopper was alone in the aisle, they bought the cheapest batteries. When either one or three people were standing next to the shopper, they were more likely to purchase a more expensive brand. When the onlookers were a group of three, the shopper always purchased the most expensive batteries.

"Impressions matter, even with complete strangers and even with a boring product," said Argo, who published her finding in the *Journal of Consumer Research* in 2005. "It's very irrational when you think about it."

Argo has a lesson for consumers trying to curb their spending. "From a consumer point of view, you need to understand how you're being influenced," Argo said. "If you want to watch your pennies, knowing the circumstances of why you splurge is important."

A Word About Falling Off the Wagon

In today's world of easy credit, few people can truly say they do not have the money to buy something they want. There's always another credit card you can get or an overdraft to dip into. You may find yourself overextending things financially speaking and regretting it later on. You really didn't have the money for it but you bought it anyway. If you can't return the item, forgive yourself and move on. Like a diet, just because you've blown one day doesn't mean all is lost. Jump back on track, and keep moving forward.

Be Prepared to Prepare

Most baby books will include lists of the items you'll need to obtain before your new arrival. Using these lists as a guideline, you can start by crossing off things you don't actually need. One book suggests you must purchase a $50 diaper bag? No need to buy that—not when you have a stylish backpack you've owned for years. Cross the diaper bag off the list! Go through the list on your own to find further examples of where you can use the things you already own in place of "baby-specific" items.

Next, start calling any and all friends who've already had children and ask them what things you don't really need. I was advised to avoid buying a change table, and buy an appropriately sized dresser instead. I could change the baby on the dresser using a $5 inflatable change pad, or on my own bed, which was a comfortable height.

Not only will friends help you cross more frivolous items off the list, but this is when they have the opportunity to let you know what items they're able to lend, give, or sell to you.

Use your common sense. Though the baby books I had say that you shouldn't have anything in the bed with the baby—such as pillows, comforters, or toys—many of the same books included bedding sets in their list of must-purchase items. Yet bedding sets for cribs often include coordinated comforters, small toys, and pillow cases—none of which you really need. It's far cheaper to purchase a few fitted sheets than an entire coordinated set that includes items you or won't even use.

Car Seats

Do you remember the golden days of your childhood, when you and seven of your best friends would pile into the family sedan to go to the bowling alley for your birthday party? Four kids wearing lap seat belts in the back (with two sharing the middle belt), two kids belted into the front passenger seat, one more kid lying across the laps in the back seat, and the smallest of the gang lying up on the shelf against the back window.

Thankfully, those days are long past. Mom no longer brings baby home from the hospital held tight against her chest. Instead, we have a strictly regulated car seat system, and before you're allowed to leave the hospital, you'll be checked for full compliance. Here's a rundown on what you need in the car.

- **Infant car seats.** These are often referred to as bucket seats, as they can easily be lifted in and out of the car easily with the handle, and be locked into a base that stays anchored in the car secured by a seatbelt or LATCH system. Infant car seats can only be used in a rear-facing mose. Most models can only be used for babies up to 20 – 22lbs.
- **Convertible seats (a.k.a three-in-ones).** These seats stay in the car permanently, and cannot be carted around. They are also used in rear-facing mode for infants, but can be switched to forward-facing mode for toddlers. Some models also convert into booster seats for older children. A small minority of families begin with the convertible seat. Starting with the bucket seat allows the convenience of carting a sleeping newborn into the house, or having somewhere they can lay while you eat dinner in a restaurant with both hands, and the convertible seat just doesn't cut it.
- **Forward-facing seats.** These seats cannot be used in rear-facing mode, and are really designed for when your child is too tall or heavy for an infant car seat. Some models of forward-facing only car seats may also convert to belt-positioning boosters for children over 40 pounds.
- **Booster seats.** These seats are for children over 40 pounds, or for a child whose stature is such that their ears have reached the top of the car seat. There are belt-positioning boosters which are high backed seats with the five point harness removed, or low back boosters.

Read your instruction manual and ensure you car seat is properly installed, the belts are snug, and baby is safe. If in doubt, check with your local fire department, insurance company, or hospital to see if they offer car seat clinics and/or car seat safety checks.

Buying a Used Car Seat

I strongly recommend buying your car seat new, or borrowing one from a trustworthy friend who can confirm it hasn't been in an accident. However, there are a few consignment shops that offer used car seats for sale. If you decide to buy a used car seat, Safe Kids Canada recommends that you check to ensure the car seat is safe using their "Safe Kids Canada Used Car Seat Checklist", which is available at <**www.safekidscanada.ca**>.

Strollers

New parents often joke that their garage is completely dedicated to stroller parking. It's rare to find a household with just one stroller. There are a number of different strollers on the market—convertible travel system strollers, mall strollers, umbrella strollers, jogging strollers or tandem strollers. You usually start with one, then graduate to others as necessary.

Most parents begin with a convertible travel system stroller. This type of stroller can be used by itself, but is initially used with the car seat locked in on top. When your baby is young, this allows you to move them from the car to the stroller without waking them (which is a nearly impossible feat to accomplish with an older baby). When your baby can sit up on their own or has outgrown the car seat component, you can use the stroller by itself. These types of strollers tend to be fairly large, so once your baby can sit up on their own, you may want to switch to a more compact mall or umbrella stroller. An umbrella stroller is ultra-lightweight, folds compactly, and usually doesn't have a basket or canopy. A mall stroller is typically an in-between type of stroller—it has a canopy and basket and more features than the umbrella stroller, but is more lightweight and manoeuvrable than the convertible travel system stroller. Both convertible travel system and mall strollers are generally sturdy, have good suspension, quality safety belts, reclining seats, washable seat padding and locking wheel brakes.

Jogging strollers work just like you would imagine—you can jog with baby in it without doing lasting damage to your child's noggin. It's probably best to wait until after the baby has arrived to determine if you'll actually use a jogging stroller. Like treadmills, they tend to work better as dust collectors than actual exercise tools. Tandem or side-by-side strollers are a must if you have twins, but if you have young children close together in age, you may just want to add a wheel board, which allows a toddler to stand on the back of the stroller when they're too tired to walk and keep up, or buy a sit-and-stand stroller—the same concept. If the oldest child is old enough, they could walk or ride their bike while baby takes a single stroller.

While necessity may dictate that you buy the cheapest stroller possible, you will find that by comparison shopping and checking out used strollers, you can often find a better used stroller for your needs than you could afford new. Better quality strollers will have nicer fabric, fully retractable or forward canopies, and they'll be easier to manoeuvre, fold, and lift.

Don't forget the add-ons, usually available second hand. Mesh baskets (to increase storage capacity), bug or rain shields, handle extenders and cup holders can all be added on for just a few dollars as and when you need them, rather than purchasing the more expensive stroller with such features already built in.

Sleep, Baby, Sleep

Where will your newborn sleep? Too often, the only place a newborn will settle down and sleep is on a parent's warm chest! At some point, you or baby will decide to sleep without constant rocking or motion, and you'll need better sleeping arrangements. Even parents who co-sleep (bring the infant in bed with them—very handy for middle of the night breastfeeding) often purchase a bedside bassinet or a special co-sleeper that allows the baby a measure of safety, and mom a degree of independence.

- **Bassinets or cradles.** These are adorable, tiny little baby beds, usually mounted on a stand. They come in all shapes and sizes, from simple little bedside cribs with a lowered side for easier access, to models that rock and vibrate. Other models are designed to be portable and lightweight. Bassinets are usually kept in the parent's bedroom until you make the transition to a crib.

  A bassinet is one item you may want to hold off buying until baby actually arrives—and keep the receipt. Why spend $200 on a rocking bassinet if your child screams like a banshee the moment you hit the rock button? Keep in mind that babies grow out of bassinets fairly quickly—as soon as they can pull themselves up a bassinet with low sides isn't safe. For some babies, this can be as young as three months.

- **Crib**. A convertible crib is a crib that converts into a toddler bed. They're expensive, especially compared to buying a simple crib or toddler bed. Often parents find it easier to switch straight from a crib to a regular single bed with an infant rail, and the toddler bed function of a convertible crib isn't ever used. If you have children close together, you'll need the crib for the new baby, and again, you won't need the toddler bed function. Should you buy a used crib? Like car seats, it can be difficult to determine if the crib is safe for use or not. Here are three things to look out for when buying a new crib:

  - How closely spaced are the slats? Slats should be no more than 2.375 inches (6 cm) apart.
  - Corner posts should be no more than 0.1 inches (3 mm) high.
  - All pieces should be intact and seem secure and sturdy.

Whatever Will Baby Wear?

A layette is a collection of clothing and bedding you'll need for your newborn. Remember that what retailers suggest you need and what you really do need are usually two very different things. How many items of clothing you need to buy will probably depend more on your laundry habits than anything else. I've always simply thrown the baby clothes in with the adult clothes, using a generic, no-name brand of detergent. I always use half the amount of detergent recommended on the box. My daughter had no adverse reactions to this practice, so her laundry was done when we had a load ready, which was once or twice a week. I'd let her wear her sleepers and onesies until she spit up over them, which meant sometimes she'd wear just one sleeper and two onesies for the whole week! I had been given a pack of seven onesies in the 0 – 3 month size and, by the time she grew out of them, she had only worn three of the seven. During her first three months she needed just three onesies, two sleepers, one pair of socks, one pair of pants, one sweater, and one frilly dress. Of course, her wardrobe was more extensive than that because of all the gift items we received, but I had to make a concerted effort to remember to dress her in those extra outfits as they weren't really required. If you find your baby is more sensitive to laundry detergent and you need to wash her clothing separately, she spits up on her clothes frequently, or has severe eczema you'll need the essential items in greater numbesr, unless you want to do laundry on a daily basis.

Money Smart Mom Tip

"Babies grow out of clothes on an almost daily basis. There were some outfits my child didn't have a chance to wear at all. Babies are more comfortable spending their days in sleepers. My boys spent most of their time in sleepers and only wore outfits when we went out. They only really needed one or two outfits at any given time. The rest is a waste."

Sera, mom of three

Pre-baby, I couldn't fathom why people would spend more money on an item of clothing for a three-month-old than they would on one for themselves! Post-baby, I completely understood the motivation. You're holding up a tiny jean jacket and hoodie combo that is so unbelievably cute you can't stand it, and you desperately want to dress your baby in that specific outfit. I'd think to myself, "Kate would look so cute in that!" Then I'd remember, "Oh right, she looks so cute in everything." And I'd put the item back on the rack—most of the time! The times when I'd cave in to the impulse and splurge, I'd always end up regretting it—usually as I was trying desperately to scrub a stubborn stain out of a gorgeous $50 hoodie. I did continue to browse the more expensive stores though—all of these stores had great clearance sections where I'd find items for a fraction of the full price, though not always with the same quality. Some stores stock $1.99 racks with clothing made specifically for that rack—

which might be shoddily made, losing embellishments or opening seams after the first wash.

Quality is important. Lesser quality sleepers literally fall apart in the wash, or get pilled and shrink, leaving no resale value to the garment. If reselling your items to consignment stores or saving them for future children is important, scout out the sales to find the best quality items available for your money.

Baby Carriers

Most babies enjoy spending as much time as possible in your arms. It's fun for the first few weeks, when no one expects you to get anything substantial accomplished anyway. But you'll soon tire of being limited to only those actions that can be done with one hand, and a baby carrier is a great way to go hands-free with baby. At chain and big box stores you can find baby carriers ranging in price from $14 to $250.

I test drove a more expensive carrier at a consignment store, and didn't notice any significant difference between it and my less expensive brand, but I do know other mothers who swear the difference is huge. At the same consignment store, I also tried out a baby sling, which I bought, and loved. I've since found slings and other carriers sold by independent stores are so much more versatile than the traditional front carriers found at the big stores, and you can use them for years, not just the first few months. If you're crafty, instructions on how to sew your own sling (or how to make one without sewing) are available at <**www.wearsthebaby. com**> or <**www.mayawrap.com/n_sewsling.php**>.

Play With Me

In the beginning, swings, vibrating chairs, exersaucers, jumpers, toy mats, activity centres, play nests, and other various toys and activities are often more for the parents than the children. Your baby isn't stimulated by her vibrating chair—she's rocked to sleep by it, giving you enough precious time to make a few bottles of formula or return a phone call. Eventually though, your baby will become more aware of her surroundings, and will begin showing real interest in activity centres and toys. Of all the products out there, which ones do you need? Which ones can you do without? It really depends on the child. While you can purchase a really elaborate vibrating chair, if your three-month-old refuses to sit in it for more than thirty seconds, it's really a waste of money.

We borrowed two big ticket items (a vibrating chair and swing) from friends, and when they needed them back after just five months, we didn't mind saying goodbye to the gear. Kate had grown tired of them, and wasn't interested in being harnessed into those contraptions anymore. We would have seriously regretted storing a very lightly used swing in the basement! Find a friend who already owns these items, and test them out with your baby. You may find you don't need to buy as many of them as you first imagined.

One of the easiest ways to create an activity centre for your baby is to spread out a soft blanket on the carpet and place a few different toys on it. If you have hard floors, use a few blankets to prevent head bangs, or look for a foam mat—some come in the form of interlocking puzzle pieces with letters or numbers on them. They'll prevent tears, and will be played with for years as your toddler learns how to attach them together and read them.

What about all these toys? Until your child is old enough to start asking for specific toys, they're usually just as happy playing with a paper bag as they are with a real toy. Expensive educational toys, while gorgeous, don't hold any greater interest for a six-month-old than the toy that comes free with a fast food meal. Yes, your daughter really loved that $40 piano toy she played with at another little girl's house, just as much as she'll really love the $5 piano you'll find at a thrift store. Trust me—they don't know the difference, and they don't care. This lesson was learned the hard way. The fun piano with the dancing monkey was thrilling at Kaylee's house. In our living room, it was apparently terrifying. Twenty bucks down the drain.

The only person who really cares is you—this season's latest, shiny new toys look nicer in your home and won't get you pitying looks from strangers at the mall. Used toys are the way to go. If the words "used toys" bring to mind threadbare teddy bears with a missing button eye, think again. These days, the quality of used toys available is exceptional. Look for brand names whose toys have obviously withstood the test of time in another child's playroom, and will surely do the same in your house.

Obviously I'm partial to buying from consignment stores—I own one! I feel consignment stores are the best place to obtain used toys year-round, but when spring thaw comes around, hitting the garage sale circuit to add to your kids' collection is a smart thing to do. Remember to run water-resistant toys through the washer or dishwasher, or give them a good scrub in the sink. Check for loose pieces that could pose a choking hazard. This is also a good practice with any new toy purchase as well—hundreds of new children's items are recalled every year for such problems.

What if you don't want to purchase any more toys for the home collection? Look to the Yellow Pages to see if your city has a toy lending library. These are toy rental services used by members to rent toys for children, usually under six years of age. Most toy libraries offer everything from wooden board puzzles to ride-on vehicles. Toys are usually rented on a two-week basis, and the cost is approximately 10% of its retail value for each toy per period.

Rub a Dub Dub—Baby in the Tub

While wandering through the baby store, you may have seen a number of different baby bath tubs or chairs for bathing your little one. If you really want one, these are items easily found in consignment stores. A few friends tell us they used theirs every night until their babies were too big for them—up to a year with some models. I found I never used the one I had borrowed. Instead, baby and I had our bath time together. I filled the tub halfway with warm water and got in with the baby. Once she was ready to get out, I'd place her in her bouncy chair lined with a towel and wrap her up. If we were alone in the house she'd sit there content until I got out and, if Keith was home he'd take her and get her ready for bed while I added hot water and soaked a bit myself.

When it comes to other bath products, you don't need special soaps or shampoos. One generic baby wash does both baby's body and hair. The cheapest baby bath toys are anything plastic that floats and that can handle soaking in water—cups are obvious toys, but plastic plates also make great smacking sounds and the big splashes that babies love.

Save Receipts, Save Packaging, Save a Few Bucks

Always keep your receipts for every baby purchase above $5. We purchased the cheapest baby monitor on the market for $19.99, and I threw away the receipt and packaging because I didn't realize anything could be wrong with a brand new baby monitor. I was right—there was nothing wrong with the monitor itself. The problem lay in what the monitor picked up— my neighbour's baby, not mine! The store wouldn't take back the monitor without the receipt or packaging, so I ended up giving it to a friend, and buying another monitor that let me listen to my child, and didn't broadcast my bad singing to the neighbours!

Mom's Layette

They say it takes nine months to put on the baby weight, and at least that long to take it all off. Even if you are successful in losing the weight, guess what? You're probably left with a body that doesn't hold much of a resemblance to your pre-baby bod. Wider feet mean any shoes that previously were comfortable are now way too tight. Your new tummy probably isn't as streamlined as it used to be, and your breasts—well, let's not get into that. Suffice it to say, you may want more support than previously required.

For some, a whole new wardrobe is in order. Scan Chapter Two again for tips on how to find new duds for less money. If you're not too far away from your previous weight, it may be beneficial to try having a seamstress resize your more expensive clothes—the cost is a fraction of the price you'll pay for new items.

Money Smart Mom Tip

"I've been a member of a kids clothing exchange for a few years, and we recently added our own clothing to the exchange. It's a great way to update your wardrobe while getting rid of stuff you no longer need or fit into."

Shannon, mom of three

Final Thought

Have you heard the old saying, "She could squeeze a dime out of a nickel?" It's one of my favourites. Try to find those categories in both baby clothing and equipment where you can pinch your pennies so hard they scream. The money left unspent can be used where your family needs it most, or can be saved for splurging on big ticket items where the extra bucks can make a big difference.

CHAPTER EIGHT

The First Year

THE FIRST YEAR WITH A new baby is an odd one. While you're showered with gifts and hand-me-downs, eliminating some of the costs involved with the new addition to your family, there's also a lot of pressure to sign up for this or that class, to take these lessons, buy those DVDs, and push that kind of stroller. There's a whole new learning curve in figuring out what works for your child. Every child is unique! You may try three different brands of bottle and nipple combinations before finding one he'll accept. There's trial and error involved in choosing which brand of diaper to use, which pacifier (if any at all), and even which laundry soap is mild on baby's skin.

Spending Money to Save Money

I used to have a bad spending habit and, even today I still find it hard to resist its siren song. When I've picked up an item on sale, my husband would ask, "How much did you spend?" Invariably I'd reply, "It was 50% off," or "I saved $35," without actually giving him a straight answer. In my opinion, I was saving the family money. In Keith's opinion, I was spending it! After I began carefully examining each purchase to determine if I had truly needed the item and had saved money on something I would have otherwise bought at a higher price, I realized Keith was right. I was spending money to save money. I'd find a great sale, and buy a $50 item for just $25. I thought I saved $25. I didn't—I'd spent $25.

Today, if I truly need a specific item and would pay more elsewhere or on another day, and if I choose to buy the item on sale, then I consider the purchase a great deal. But pulling out my wallet never means saving money – it means spending it. You save money when you put it in a bank account, an investment, an RRSP, or an RESP, never when you give it to a department store.

A low price is not necessarily always a good deal. If you'll be putting that shirt or pair of skates on a credit card, then not paying that credit card off at the end of the month, a $50 item could cost you $60 or more by the time it's paid off. So is the item still a good deal at $60?

Bottles and ...

One of the most sensitive parenting topics should always be, in my opinion, a private decision between a mother and her baby. However, breastfeeding has long been a hot topic among parenting experts, medical authorities, moms, dads, and childless adults alike.

Because I chose not to breastfeed my first child after much difficulty in figuring it all out, I felt immense pressure from other mothers and medical experts in feeding Kate at the mall, or when the issue arose in discussion groups or parenting websites. I don't have any problems with encouraging breastfeeding—what I don't like is the not-so-subtle campaign to dismiss the concerns of mothers who have difficulty breastfeeding, and to belittle mothers who choose, for whatever reason, not to breastfeed. Contrary to most pro-breastfeeding literature, not everyone finds breastfeeding natural, easy, or wonderful. In fact, many women find it excruciatingly painful, physically impossible, or they simply don't like it, however easy it is for them. Adoptive mothers have been known to breastfeed adopted children, but only with much advance preparation, which is not always possible. Often we are our own worst enemies—women will claim that yes, they hurt too, but all you have to do is keep going and it soon will be problem-free. It may be true for them, but it doesn't apply to everyone.

With my second child, I was determined to try again. I found the process even harder than the first time, and again I heard over and over, "You just have to get used to it—it can't be that bad." I snapped, "Listen, I gave birth to this nearly nine-pound baby without drugs—and nursing hurts more!" But this time I made an appointment with a lactation specialist. She offered techniques, tools, and a diagnosis of tied tongue, and within days nursing was bliss, not torture. Instead of spending hundreds and hundreds of dollars on bottles, formulas and pumps, the odd can of formula was able to sustain Jacqueline whenever I went out until she switched to whole milk.

Marketing campaigns aside, exclusive breastfeeding isn't necessarily cheap. You might want to buy nursing bras and shirts, nursing pads and, if you ever want more than four hours away from baby, a breast pump and bottles, plus a can or two of formula. Breastfeeding is less expensive than formula feeding, but it's not necessarily free.

Basically, there are two kinds of breast pumps on the market, the manual and the electric. Manual pumps are inexpensive, but not terribly effective—it can take three to four times as long to pump the same amount of milk manually as can be achieved with an electric pump. If you rarely pump, a manual pump is the most cost-effective option. However, if you need to pump so you can have time away from baby for work or other reasons, or you find you have to pump to stimulate milk production, an electric pump is often the answer. Purchasing a good electric pump outright is costly—the cheapest ones cost about $75. You may be able to find a used unit at a consignment store, through a classified advertisement or via a local parenting website, but secondhand breast pumps are not generally recommended as there exists a slight risk of infection or the transmission of illness. You can also rent electric breast pumps from large drugstore chains—they generally cost between $40 and $60 a month. These commercially rented machines are built to ensure there is no risk of the transmission of illness. Economically, if you end up using a pump for six months it would have been more cost-effective to buy a new unit. An expensive manual pump might work better than an inexpensive electric pump—it's difficult to know which pump will work best for your body.

Purchasing a breast pump is a decision you should make after baby arrives, once you've figured out if you will be breastfeeding, and what your pump requirements are likely to be.

When it comes to buying bottles, there are plenty of options available. Like many other consumer products, I suggest trying the least expensive brand first and seeing if they are satisfactory. I liked the cheapest bottles on the market, while some friends relied on the more expensive brands said to reduce air bubbles while drinking, thereby reducing gas and other digestive problems. Don't buy too many bottles or nipples—it's quick and easy enough to clean them after use in hot soapy water, or sterilize them in an inexpensive microwave steam sterilizer if you wish. Babies also require nipples with different sized holes, for slow, medium or fast flow. Start with slow flow nipples and move up as baby demands—we never did make it to the fast ones. By the time your child is ready for fast flow nipples they may also be ready to say goodbye to bottles and transition to sippy cups.

In 2008, the Canadian government announced it would be the first country to ban Bisphenol A (BPA) in baby bottles. BPA is an estrogenic hormone disrupter that causes reproductive damage and may lead to prostate and breast cancer in adulthood. Whether the levels of BPA leached in baby bottles is high enough to have such an effect is still under debate. However, most parents are practicing a better-safe-than-sorry policy. Canadian stores no longer carry baby bottles containing BPA, but you can often find them at garage sales, or some might be handed down to you. If you choose to use bottles and you're unsure of the BPA content, it would be prudent to avoid heating the bottles or pouring boiling water into them.

Bottoms

Ask any frugal parent how to save money with a baby, and almost always they'll mention cloth diapers. Savings estimates, depending on what type of diaper is used, range from $1,000 to $2,000 over a three-year period. The overall savings continue to grow when parents reuse cloth diapers for two or three children. The study by the Home Economics Department at Manitoba Agriculture—mentioned in Chapter One—estimates the cost of clothing for each year including the cost of cloth diapers. The same survey states that, "if disposable diapers were used instead of cloth diapers, the additional expense for two and one half years of using diapers (*including reduced laundering costs*) would be $1,345." The estimated savings is $1663.60 for the first child alone.

To save even more money, some industrious parents even make their own diapers. If you're interested in trying your hand at diaper making, visit <**www.borntolove.com**> for full instructions.

In examining the issue of cloth versus disposable diapers, we're back to the convenience factor. Though lugging around humongous packs of disposable diapers and storing them is anything but convenient, actually using them is quick and simple. When the diaper's used, it's simply popped into a trash bin. Cloth diapers are definitely more work, but probably not as much as you might think. In a cloth diapering system, there's more of an initial outlay in cost, as you'll require two to three dozen absorbent diapers and six waterproof covers in each size your baby will need.

When purchasing cloth diapers, you can buy prefolds that require pins for less than $2 each. The more complex diapers are fitted diapers with snaps or Velcro and cost around $8 to $25 or more each, but are much easier to use, especially for babysitters or other caregivers not familiar with cloth diapers.

Cleaning cloth diapers is not that much more disgusting than dealing with disposables. Either way, you simply dump the solids into the toilet—a practice also recommended for disposables but not often followed—then wash the cloth diapers in the washing machine following the instructions provided when you purchased your diapers.

Like most parenting advice, much of the evidence to support either method of diapering is contradictory. Some experts claim cloth diapers prevent diaper rash while others claim their use causes increased diaper rash. Environmental studies have determined that there is no clear winner when it comes to the cloth versus disposable debate. Cloth diapers require more energy and water consumption, while disposables pollute landfills. If you choose to use cloth, keep in mind that some daycares won't accept babies in cloth diapers, so you may have to buy a limited supply of disposables. When travelling, use disposables—pity the poor airport security officer who has to check a plastic bag full of dirty cloth diapers!

If you want to use cloth diapers, but can't or don't want to wash them yourself, research the price of a diaper service in your city. Most delivery services drop off clean cloth diapers and pick up the dirty ones at your doorstep every week or two. The cost for such a service is about the same price as buying disposables.

Ultimately, you should choose the diapering system that is best suited to your lifestyle, budget, and personal preferences.

Diaper Data

- In the first two years, the average baby will require between 5,000 to 7,000 diaper changes.
- Over four million disposable diapers are discarded in Canada per day.
- About 85% of Canadian parents use disposable diapers.
- Washing a load of diapers once or twice a week is roughly equivalent to flushing a toilet five times a day for a week.

Yum Mum! Making Your Own Baby Food

Whether you're breast or bottle feeding, after several months of an all-liquid diet, your baby will be ready to chow down on a little solid food. Around six months of age you can add iron-fortified baby cereals, which may be a staple in their diet for many months to come.

Once baby is comfortable with cereal, you can begin introducing fruit and vegetables into their diet. If you've checked out the jars of baby food in the supermarket, you may question why you're paying $0.50 for $0.05 worth of carrots. Or maybe you got a whiff of a jar of baby peas and wondered how companies could make peas and water smell so unappetizing. If so, you may be considering testing your culinary skills by making your own baby food. It might seem daunting, but making your own baby food is quick, cost-effective, and rewarding.

Preparing baby food takes very little time, effort, and money. All you need is a blender or food processor, a steamer basket, and a few ice cube trays. Pick up a few vegetables and fruits—broccoli, carrots, cauliflower, peas, sweet potatoes, apples, mango—anything except citrus fruits will do. Clean and peel the food, steam it in separate batches, and then puree it in a blender or food processor until it is smooth. Add water, if necessary, for a smoother consistency. Spoon the purees into ice cube trays, cover with plastic wrap, and freeze. Once frozen, dump the cubes into labelled freezer bags—they'll keep for up to three months. In less than two hours, you can make enough food for baby for a month. A small manually operated food mill can be useful for small portions, or for using at restaurants, especially when travelling.

To prepare food from frozen, remove the required cubes and thaw them overnight in a small container in the fridge. Initially baby may only eat half a cube or less, but will soon move up to a cube or two or even more of different foods.

As baby grows, you can begin serving them combination meals. But skip the elaborate baby recipes—simply puree the healthy meals you've made for the rest of your family. Beef stew, chicken casserole, lasagna—a few servings from your balanced family meals will feed baby for a month or two.

There are many benefits to making your own baby food. You can trim between $10 to $15 a month off your food budget, or more as baby consumes more. Quality and taste are also among the reasons most parents give for making their own baby food. Though baby food marketed to young babies have no added sugars and starchy fillers, the foods designed for older babies do contain these items, lowering their nutritional value. By making your own baby food, you'll also have greater control over what your children eat, and their taste buds can be exposed to foods the rest of the family already enjoys. You'll also make fewer trips to the grocery store, saving yourself the hassle of lugging home and then recycling all those little jars.

A few tips for making baby food:

- Always practice safe food handling procedures.
- Scrub fruits and vegetables very well with a vegetable brush.
- Soft fruits like bananas need only be mashed; hard fruits should be cooked first.
- Trim excess fat off poultry and meat.
- Steam the vegetables, don't boil them.
- Don't add salt and sugar.

In larger cities across Canada you can usually find companies selling organic, wholesome baby food in cubes just like the ones you can make yourself, generally at a cost of $2 – 4 a day. While it would be fun to tell the other moms, "Oh, this? It's just wild mushroom ricotta with sugar snap peas," if you're reading this book you probably aren't interested in signing up for weekly delivery of such foods. However, you could consider joining with a few other moms whose babies are the same age as yours and trying a few more elaborate recipes—you can share the results and each go home with a wider variety than you would probably prepare by yourself.

Money Smart Mom Tip

"I enjoy cooking and also looked into making my own baby food as a way to save money. I had also tasted the jarred baby foods and I was not too keen on the taste. To me, they do not taste at all like the real thing. I wanted my daughter to learn to eat green beans that taste like green beans. It is very important not to raise a picky eater. By making her baby food myself, I'm hoping to avoid that and so far I think I have. Some people have the perception that I must be a 'granola-crunching, only eat organic foods' person. That is a common misconception and I'm hoping that more people will have the courage to try to make their own baby food too!"

Amanda, mom of one

A Room With a View

Where will baby sleep? Even parents who co-sleep need to spend a few bucks to purchase something to protect their new baby from a sound sleeping spouse's accidental roll. Purchasing a basic in-bed co-sleeper (a small infant bed with half walls around most of the bed) will also enable the parents to rest easier and without fear. More elaborate co-sleepers, which are basically bassinets with drop down sides, can be rolled up and connected to the side of the parent's bed, a good but more expensive option for those without much room in their bed.

Recommended Reading

Reading **The Baby's Table: Over 150 Easy, Healthy and Homemade Recipes Your Baby Will Love** *by Brenda Bradshaw and Dr. Lauren Donaldson Bramley while I was pregnant convinced me that preparing my own baby food was the way to go. Though a significant portion of the recipes are easily figured out on your own (mashed bananas, steamed vegetables, etc.), it's the additional sidebars I found helpful. When do you start introducing specific fruits? How do you prepare an apple so it's safe for baby to eat? What should you do if your child refuses certain foods? Bradshaw and Bramley have all the answers in this easy-to-read book.*

Purchasing a crib, whether it's set up in their own room, yours, or an older sibling's, should be done with care and attention. Follow the guidelines mentioned in Chapter Seven for buying a used crib. Should you buy a crib that converts to a toddler bed? That depends. While sales are still strong for these kinds of cribs, if you have your children close together, the next one might need the crib before the first is ready to move out of it, and the first won't ever get to use the toddler bed option. Also, a toddler bed is not essential—a low single twin bed with a bed rail is perfectly fine for sleeping arrangements after the child has outgrown their crib.

While the adjustment period might be tough, you can bunk kids in the same room if you don't have as many extra bedrooms as you have children. Most kids are fine with sharing a room with siblings, and some do right up until their teenage years.

Brilliant Babies

Honestly, if this generation of babies doesn't solve world hunger or institute world peace, I think we could successfully sue baby product manufacturers. Whether it's an educational DVD, flash cards or baby sign language, there are hundreds of educational products and programs with marketing ploys designed to make moms feel like their baby will flunk preschool if he didn't spend his first twelve months of life learning sign language, being massaged by a registered infant massage therapist, or attending mommy-and-me gym and music classes.

If your baby loves those simplistic baby DVDs, by all means, purchase enough titles to get yourself half an hour's peace to make supper or read a magazine. Borrow from friends or the library, or scour the consignment shops—just don't buy the 10 DVD set brand-new. Babies and toddlers love routine—she's probably just as happy watching the same one over and over again.

A Year to Remember

It's no surprise that many new moms take up scrapbooking as a hobby— what better way to commemorate the unforgettable moments than with a personalised storybook? But scrapbooking, along with creating and sending birth announcements, can quickly get expensive. If you love the hobby, look for complete kits—they're always cheaper than buying paper supplies and embellishments separately. Don't invest too much in the tools—you may find your interest waning when you have toddlers to run after. Many scrapbooking stores hold open house nights where you can pay a small fee and come and use their expensive cutters and other tools all evening in a special room with plenty of table space. Bring a few good friends and leave your wallet in the car so you won't be tempted to buy that divine $9 roll of ribbon that so perfectly matches the dress in that Easter photo.

What about cameras and camcorders? I do think it's important to have a good digital camera for capturing your baby's childhood, and both advances in technology and market penetration have both helped to significantly reduce the cost of this kind of equipment. You can now get a decent digital camera for under $150, and then be selective about which photos you print, emailing them instead of printing and mailing copies to every aunt, cousin, and grandparent. In my opinion, a camcorder isn't vital to own, especially if you can find a friend willing to lend you theirs once in awhile. We received an easy-to-use, compact little camcorder as a gift, and still only manage to use it a few times a year. Your digital camera may also have the ability to record short videos of decent quality. While you may have thousands of photos of your children, have you also recorded some of the things that can't be captured on film? The way you felt the first time they laughed, how everyone reacted the first time they repeated your favourite curse word at Sunday dinner? These are moments than can only be expressed through the written word, so grab a pen and journal, or open your word processing program and write down your thoughts about your children and what they're doing. These letters to them should be kept for your own rereading later and for their own eventual reading too.

> I bought an inexpensive journal for each of my children and made a point of writing in them from time to time. My son is now 21 and I still write in his! When I have grandkids, I will give the journals to my children so they can read my thoughts about their childhood.
>
> *Joan, mom of two*

Babysitting Blues

No matter how enamoured you are of your precious baby, it might still be a good idea to spend some time away, either by yourself or with your partner. I've met parents who have never been away from their nine-month-old for more than the time it takes to shower, and others who've left newborns for sleepovers with grandma almost from day one. How much time you need or want away from your little one will be influenced by the kind of babysitting you can find and afford. Even if you don't particularly need the time to yourself, you may want to use the occasional babysitter to get your child used to being cared for by someone other than mom to make transitioning to child care easier if you go back to work.

How do you find reliable babysitters, and how much will they cost? I remember making $4 an hour for three or more kids years ago, and being trusted with caring for newborns before I had even hit my teens. These days, it doesn't seem as though many teenage girls are as interested in making money through babysitting, and those that do charge astronomical rates. If all you need is the occasional evening out and have no family willing to come and help for free, you could try posting an ad at your local recreational centre or high school.

Babysitting Co-op

If you have a few friends in the same situation, looking for occasional care but not wanting to take out a loan for it, why not try a babysitting co-op? If your community doesn't have one yet, they're actually relatively easy to start and coordinate.

First, you need to get a core group of parents involved, and establish your guidelines for sits. Will you use tokens or points as "payment"? What responsibilities are required on the part of the sitter in terms of snacks and lunches? You'll need to create rules around driving, cancellations, late or early pickups, the number and age of the children, discipline, etc. Most groups hold monthly meetings where various issues are discussed and problems resolved as a group. Groups may advertise by word of mouth, or by using a local parenting website.

Babysitting co-ops can be especially helpful for moms working part-time. With drop-in daycare for two kids in my city costing $80 a day, a parent needing just three days of care a month is looking at a bill of $240 a month for child care. By using a babysitting co-op, she skips the hefty fees in exchange for just a few days of caring for someone else's kids. If you already have children, you know that often caring for a few more kids is easier than caring for just your own! When your child has a friend over, often they need far less of your attention than if they were home alone with just you.

The *Today's Parent* website <**www.todaysparent.com**> has a fantastic resource for anyone wanting to start a babysitting co-op, including forms, guidelines, etc. You could also pick up *Smart Mom's Babysitting Co-op Handbook*, by Gary Myers.

A mom of three, Angela joined her local babysitting co-op when her twins were just four-months-old. In the five years since joining, she estimates that she's saved over $1,000 in babysitting. "Best of all, I have met some incredibly wonderful women that I would not otherwise have had an opportunity to meet. To me this is one of the most wonderful parts of the co-op," says Angela.

Final Thought

The first year with your first baby can be an expensive one if you blindly buy every product pushed on you by overeager baby store clerks, or sign up for every available mommy-and-me class. It's more important than ever to create and stick to a budget. Even the most frugal first time mom will get a laugh out of the purchases she thought were absolute necessities when subsequent babies arrive to far less fanfare and far fewer classes!

CHAPTER NINE

To Preschool

YOUR ADORABLE NEWBORN HAS SOMEHOW morphed into a walking, talking, possibly tyrannical toddler. No longer content to spend hours in swings or slings, they want to be entertained, and you're entertaining the thought of having more!

Every Last Class

While I enjoyed some of the classes I took with my daughter, there were others where I ended up skipping three quarters of the sessions. Sometimes signing up for a swimming lesson was a means of ensuring I'd get out to the pool when I'd otherwise skip it. I hate pools, but Kate loves them, so it ensured I'd get my post-baby body into a swimsuit (horror of horrors) at least once a week. Many classes offer a free first visit, and that initial exposure was enough to let me decide if the class was worth joining.

Keep in mind that the classes and lessons and all of the other wonderfully enriching experiences for very young children are generally a first baby, first year journey and expense. Though there are some classes which cater to both baby and toddler participation, once you have two tots in tow, the last thing you'll probably have the time or energy for is driving across the city to sing to your six-month-old while you keep an eye on your rambunctious toddler, something you can do at home with a Raffi CD with far less effort and a bit less cost.

Avoiding a Scrooge Reputation

Birthdays, graduations, housewarmings, Christmas—it seems like every month includes events requiring the purchase of gifts for other people. Gift giving is a time-honoured tradition, and one loaded with equal amounts of love and guilt. Guilt about what you're spending and what other people have spent on you. It can take the fun right out of the occasion.

I once stumbled across a website that dealt with the issue of Christmas gift giving, and how to find ways to save while giving. One tip encouraged readers to get a holiday job to ensure they could afford the gifts they wanted to give! I was shocked. Is this what Christmas is about? What do you think your loved ones want—a better gift, or more time with you?

Here are a few ways to deal with gift giving all year round.

- **Trim Your List.** You might be in a cycle of exchanging gifts with immediate and extended family, friends, and work acquaintances. Now is the perfect time to wean some people out of the gift circle. Be honest—let them know you simply can't afford to spend so much money on gifts every year, and you'll now only be buying for immediate family. Send them a personal card instead.
- **Start a New Tradition.** If you have numerous family members for whom you have traditionally bought gifts at Christmas, see if they'd be interested in a gift exchange, or in drawing names for gifts. If you're a family of bargain hunters, why not exchange gifts after a late dinner on Boxing Day instead? You can buy your gifts that morning and wrap them in the afternoon (with Christmas wrap bought at 75% off). Stop buying birthday presents for your siblings and send them framed photos of their nieces or nephews instead, or host a birthday dinner for them.
- **List it.** Decide what you can afford to spend on gifts, and then select the gifts. You may find it easiest to create a list, take out the amount in cash, and do your shopping in one afternoon. If you have the willpower, shop for those on your list all year round at times when great items go on sale. Keep a list in your wallet or

on your computer so you have a plan of what you want to buy for whom, and how much you can afford to spend.

- **Don't Compete.** If your older brother buys your parents a trip to Jamaica, give them an indoor tanning package, new beach towels, or extra film and batteries. He's rich, but you're thoughtful.
- **Receive Graciously.** Don't give $5 gifts but drop hints that you want an XBox for your birthday. Appreciate the thought behind the gifts you receive and don't judge them on their monetary value.
- **Sit This One Out.** Often parents will invite every child in a class to their child's birthday party in order to not exclude anyone. If your child isn't desperate to attend, skip it and hang out as a family instead. Unlike weddings, if you can't make the party, you don't have to send a gift for birthday celebrations you don't attend—a card will suffice.
- **All Things are Not Equal.** If you snagged a great deal on a few toys with the idea of giving them as gifts, resist the temptation to continue buying until you've reached a specific dollar value. If the toy was originally $30 who has to know that you got it for $6? Score! Don't keep buying more to reach some elusive, unspoken, birthday party gift value requirement.

Wallet-Saving Gift Ideas

- Create coupons for help with spring cleaning or babysitting.
- Videotape your parents talking about childhood memories and give the tape to siblings or grand children.
- Make a calendar with pictures of family members. Mark it with important family birthdays and anniversaries.
- When was the last time you had your portrait taken with your brothers and sisters? Get your siblings together and have your photo taken at an inexpensive photo studio—the prices are perfect, and you get a load of photos.
- Assemble the recipes for your family favourites and print a recipe collection for everyone in the family.
- Buy a used book and in the inside cover explain why you chose the book for that person.

- Do you remember your favourite childhood books? Your parents likely remember reading them to you. Buy them a copy, and be sure to inscribe it.

- Create a family website where siblings, parents, cousins, and other relatives around the world can post photos, announcements, and update each other on their lives.

- Looking for a gift the kids won't lose interest in within a day? Little kids love costumes, so create a Tickle Trunk! Buy a large, sturdy plastic container, and visit a thrift store for inexpensive and unusual costume pieces.

- Create themed gift baskets. Cold weather baskets can contain hot chocolate, soup mixes, and warm socks; a movie basket can contain popcorn, soda, candy, and a previously viewed movie.

- Plan a romantic dinner for two and present your honey with a menu, asking them to make a reservation soon.

- If you've received a nice gift that simply isn't useful to you, feel free to re-gift it to someone who might find it more useful. Just be sure not to give it back to the person that gave it to you, or someone else they know!

- Craft kits can be pricey, and full of junky stuff kids won't use. Create a basic travel craft kit from dollar store items.

- Take a look around the recipient's home to see if you can find anything that needs replacing and keep your ear to the ground about what they might need. Are their slippers in rough shape? Are they always remarking about how they have to buy a hammer?

- Got a foodie on your list? Buy them a small, top-quality kitchen tool, like a new spatula or whisk.

- How crafty are you? If you're so inclined, homemade gifts are a gift from the heart (and hands). You may be able to knit baby clothes, frame your beautiful photographs inexpensively, make stockings, or create one-of-a-kind Christmas ornaments.

- Find strangely shaped cookie cutters that will appeal to a friend's sense of humour.

- Magazine subscriptions are inexpensive, and it's like the recipient receives a gift every month!

- Instead of spending $40 on a new board game, invest $10 in an old classic, and pair it with a promise for a fun night of games and conversation.
- A spa day gift is out of the question, but you can give a loved one the spa experience at home. Pick up bubble bath, a bath sponge, candle, and make a relaxing CD to top it off.
- Thoughtful gifts are always appreciated, even if they're small. Give a reader a selection of funny bookmarks, a writer a few gel pens, and a whiteboard for a forgetful friend.
- Small denomination gift certificates to a friend's favourite coffee house will be appreciated.
- With a little planning, you can give beautiful houseplants in yard sale plant pots just using cuttings from your own plants.
- Create cookies in a jar. Measure out the dry ingredients for your favourite cookie recipe, and layer in a glass jar. Write out the complete recipe, along with instructions on preparing the mix on a pretty card, and decorate the jar with a festive ribbon.
- Dollar stores are great places to find inexpensive wrapping paper or gift bags, but your least expensive alternative is to buy a large roll of white or brown craft paper from an art supply store and have the kids decorate it with stamps, stickers and crayons.

Recommended Reading

- *Gifts from the Kitchen* by Jean Paré
- *Gifts Kids Can Make* by Sheila McGraw
- *Gifts for the Family: Over 120 Projects to Make for Those You Love in Under 30 Minutes* by Editors of Reader's Digest
- *Christmas Presents Kids Can Make* by Kathy Ross

Birthday Budget Busting

Speaking of gifts, birthday parties can be a big blow to your monthly budget. It seems like the most elaborate and expensive birthday parties are thrown for kids so young they'll never remember it! As they get older, your kids are actually less likely to want elaborate entertainment or ultra-coordinated decor. Even if you're not in a circle of friends all trying to outdo the efforts of others with their birthday party bashes, your spending on these shindigs can quickly get out of control. Look for inexpensive or free venues. Summer parties can be held in your backyard, or at a local park with a covered picnic area. Check your local kiddie play places—they might offer packages that will be close to what you'd spend on a home party, with a lot less work and stress.

Hosting a themed birthday can keep things cheap and creative. Go with a generic theme of race cars or pirates instead of Disney princesses or other television or movie characters. Forgo the grocery store specialty cake or divinely decorated cake shop cake in favour of a basic sheet cake made with a boxed mix, and topped with dollar store figurines that match the party's theme. A borrowed bounce house will be a hit with younger kids, and you can create games and crafts that match the party theme from ideas found on online sites that will cost little or nothing to implement. Get creative with the decor by making decorations yourself, and enlist the help of the birthday child.

Loot bags can be one of the most expensive parts of any child's party. Keep an eye out, year round, for items that would work well as loot bag fillers, or as single item party favours. Check big box stores selling off summer toys at clearance prices—often things like outdoor vinyl bounce balls can be snagged for under $1 each, as can large outdoor chalk tubs.

Dealing with the "Gimmies"

When you were pregnant with your first child, you were probably convinced that you would not spend scads of cash on every primary coloured object your child fancied. Now that you have one or more children, sometimes your home looks like it was corporately sponsored by a toy store.

No parent wants their child to feel deprived, but they also usually don't want to raise an overindulged child. Yet when the aisles of the toy department are filled with your childhood favourites and other items you're sure your little one will delight in playing with, it's hard to maintain control. Toss just a few items into the cart, and there goes your pay cheque.

The older they get, the smarter they get. While it didn't seem like a big deal that you bought your toddler a special treat every time you went grocery shopping, or a small toy every time you visited a toy store, you'll soon find that "special treat" has become a mandatory purchase. Keep it up and at the end of the year you'll find a garbage bag's worth of little junky toys that cost you more than you'll care to think about. Setting the precedent of a reward with every store you visit is a really bad idea. And frankly, it's not fair to your kids either, because one of these days you're going to want to curtail this spending from your budget, and your kids are going to have a hard time with the transition.

Selling Your Stuff

In Chapter Seven I talked about shopping at consignment stores and finding other, more economic, sources for buying used baby gear. Now it's time for the real scoop on the best way to sell your stuff to make the most money. Though I'll specifically address kids gear, you may find unused household goods lying around that could net you a few bucks as well.

Consignment or Resale

A consignment store sells used items on consignment for customers— the store reviews the items dropped off, selects what they think will sell, prices everything and keeps track of whose items are sold in order to pay out the consigners. Generally a consignment store will pay you between 30% and 50% of what the item sells for. Consignment stores keep the items for a specific number of days (usually 60) with a scheduled markdown and a return policy for unsold items. You may be required to search through the racks to find your items (they give you a list) or they might pull them out for you. Items not wanted back are given to local charity. Money you earn can usually be cashed out or used as store credit anytime—but every store has a different policy, so make sure you read the agreement carefully and that you understand the whole process before you sign it.

A resale store (called a buy outright shop in the industry) will review items brought in on the spot or within a few days, and make you an offer for the batch. Because resale stores are assuming more risk than a consignment store (an item they buy from you for $8 may end up being cleared out for $1 when no one wanted it) they offer you a lower percentage of the initial price they will put on your items, generally between 15% and 30%. While you'll probably walk away with less money for you possessions at a resale shop, you don't have to go back to collect your money, or wait until your items sell in order to be paid—you walk out with cash in hand. Some stores may only offer store credit for certain items.

Consignment and resale shops only stay in business and flourish by providing what their shoppers want, and that's not perfectly matched with what consigners want to bring in. I've had people try and drop off broken toys, thirty-year-old baby equipment, white t-shirts with crusted spaghetti sauce covering the front, even unclean potties. No matter how unsaleable, unusable, or flat out revolting an item is, some people just don't understand why no one wants these items. Don't be offended if a store turns your favourite baby outfit away—they may simply have too many similar outfits in stock, not had success in selling the brand in the past, or it may be that the style of the garment is no longer what moms are looking for. The next store you visit may be looking for just that outfit—every store has a different clientele and, with an average consignment or resale store selling between 600 and 3,000 items per week, they know better than anyone what will and will not appeal to their customer base.

Garage Sales

Holding a successful garage sale requires a lot of work, but it can be a fun social event with your neighbours and raise you some instant cash. A garage sale is one way you can get rid of unwanted items—not just those from the nursery—or things consignment and resale stores aren't interested in taking.

The best way to attract a lot of attention to your garage sale is to join forces with your neighbours. At least a month before you want to hold the sale, contact your neighbourhood association—if you have one, or deliver a flyer to the homes in your neighbourhood both advertising the sale and to see who else wants to have a garage sale at the same time. If everyone pitches in a small amount of money you can run a few classified advertisements in the garage sale section of your local newspaper, remembering to mention that it's a huge multi-street garage sale. Get the sale posters up the night before with clear directions and you'll be amazed at the volume of traffic your normally quiet residential street will experience.

When holding a garage sale, price your items cheaply and be willing to bargain—it's part of the fun. Put large items by the road to tempt passers-by to park and come and see your wares, and move your vehicles to permit the best parking available. Turn on the stereo to avoid awkward silences while shoppers browse, ensure you have a good cash float (kept on you at all times), and recruit any older children you might have to help. This is a great opportunity to engage younger children who can host an old-fashioned lemonade stand, or better yet, offer muffins, coffee, and chilled cans of pop at a good mark-up!

Community Sales

Many communities, churches, and local organizations (such as twins and triplets clubs) hold baby sales annually or biannually. Every group runs their sale differently depending on the size of the event. You may be required to rent a table space from which to sell your items, and be responsible for having your own change, bags, and often set up and take down your table. At larger events you may simply have to tag your items beforehand with specially created tags that identify your name and the price of each piece. The organizers hold the sale, setting it up with the help of volunteers (who usually take a larger percentage of profit from their sale items in return for this donation of time). You can expect to receive between 60% to 80% of the sale price of your items.

Baby sales can be intense—at the good ones, people line up for hours just to be the first through the doors. Shoppers are expecting bargain-basement pricing though, so price your items accordingly, or they will be the only ones left behind at the end of the day. Often the group organized sales have an across the board 50%-off-after-2:00 pm type of policy to ensure they don't have too many items to sort or donate after the event.

Classifieds and Online Websites

The rise in popularity of free, online classified websites have virtually killed off the more traditional print media classified advertisements section as a way to sell relatively inexpensive items—such as general household items and baby clothing or equipment. Selling items online means putting up with strangers phoning and emailing, some of whom won't show up. Buying from websites like these means driving all around your city and knocking on stranger's doors. Some of the downsides I've experienced are the item not the same as described online, the seller not being home when they said they would be, or the item is sold to someone while I was en route and the seller didn't call my cell phone number to save me the trip. Conversely, I've scored a few great finds via online sites, such as our retro black leather couch for under $100. I keep checking these websites for great deals on things we really do need.

A couple of suggestions when using online websites:

- If you're selling items on these websites, accept cash only—no cheques, no money orders. There is a widely-used scam where buyers give you a money order or cheque or bank draft for more money than you've asked for the item and they ask you to send or give them a money order for the difference. By the time the cheque bounces or the money order or bank draft is discovered as a fake, you're out the real money you sent them.
- If you're home alone, or alone with your children, don't invite anyone to your home. Ensure another adult is in the home with you, or agree to make the swap somewhere public on neutral ground.

Final Thought

Now is definitely the time to recognize that your toddler is just as content with a dollar store toy as they would be with a high end item at forty times the price. Soon they're going to start being impacted by television commercials and school friends, and the demands for more expensive stuff will begin. If you don't have a good handle on your family finances yet, and still aren't sure where your money is going or how to tackle your debt and savings plans, you can't wait any longer. The stakes are raised once your kids hit school, and you need to be prepared.

CHAPTER TEN

As They Grow

I'M STARTING THIS CHAPTER WITH a general overview about teaching your kids about money, because it's the foundation of dealing with the many needs and wants they will throw at you over the next few years. Whether it's involvement in sports, designer clothing, sleep-away camps or elaborate birthday parties, now is when the control of your spending on your children is under siege. It's easy to buy used clothing for a baby who can't talk back and wouldn't know the difference from new anyway; it's quite another thing to convince a ten-year-old to wear hand-me-down sneakers when all the cool kids in his class are wearing the latest in brand-name runners.

Raising Money-Smart Kids

Do you know how much money your parents made when you were growing up? How much they had saved in their RRSP? If you're like most people, you probably don't know the specifics concerning your parent's finances as a child. Maybe you suspected there wasn't enough, after hearing your parents complain about grocery bills, or turn you down when you asked for money for a new videogame. You may have even heard the old, "Do you think money goes on trees?" a few times, or worse, "We can't afford that," or "We don't have enough money for that." While it's a quick and easy answer to deliver to the four-year-old tugging at your sleeve for a new toy, it doesn't help kids learn good money management skills, and won't help the next time they want something.

If you want your kids to grow up with a healthy understanding of how money affects their lives, money should not be a taboo subject in your home. As soon as your children begin to show signs of grasping the concept of money, you can think about introducing an allowance, and talking about the concepts of earning money, saving it, and spending it. The details about discussing earning and spending are covered under the heading Play Money, but for now I'm talking about the bigger picture, and the idea of discussing your family's financial situation.

When talking to your kids about your personal finances, it's important to be honest, but it's also crucial to avoid scaring your kids. Talk about money as a family at the dinner table or during a family meeting, not in the middle of a toy store. If you and your spouse are not on the same page about financial issues, you need to sort this out first. Arguing about money in front of your children will send entirely the wrong message.

If you've been facing a lot of pressure from your children every time they watch television commercials or whenever they come home from an indulged friend's house, sit down as a family and discuss those pressures. Talk to them about *needs* versus *wants*, and how you make a certain income each month that is not infinite. Are you putting money away for your retirement and their education? Tell them this. Reassure them that just because you're choosing not to put video game purchases on your credit card or planning an expensive vacation on credit, doesn't mean you will not have money for important things like food and shelter. Don't say you can't afford something—say you're choosing not to spend money on it and are choosing to spend your money on something else.

It can help to also focus on the enjoyable things you do as a family that do not cost money. This is a valuable activity for your spouse and you as well. When you sit down to talk to your kids about having fun without spending money, they may surprise you with their own ideas. Often, it's a matter of just getting off the couch. It's easy to spend $80 and take the kids to the movies on a Sunday afternoon—it's a little more work to plan a picnic in the park and take your frisbees and kites. As you reconnect with your family during activities that don't require spending money, you'll find you enjoy these times more than you expected.

Play Money

Teaching your children about the practical side of money usually starts with introducing an allowance. A general rule of thumb is to budget one dollar per year per week, multiplied by the age of the child. So your five-year-old would receive $5 a week, your seven-year-old $7 a week. Many parenting experts say allowances should not be tied to chores, and chores are simply part of being in the family, and must be done regardless. But in real life, not handing over an allowance because toys weren't picked up and beds weren't made is a pretty common consequence.

Should you force your child to save a certain percentage of their allowance or income? I think so, and I liken it to the CPP. It's deducted for their own good, whether they like it or not. Set a percentage to deduct, and tuck it away in their RESP. It might be small change, but it's the principle of the idea that matters.

Regardless of whether you insist on savings, you should take your children to your financial institution to set up a bank account in their name. They'll be thrilled with the process, and it can help to encourage savings. Of course, the natural end to savings for children is the buying! What do you do when your child wants to spend their savings on something you think they'll ultimately regret buying? It's good to talk to them about the pros and cons of their buying decisions, but ultimately you should leave the decision up to them. If they have buyer's remorse, use it as a learning opportunity.

Going Back to Work

Once your children start going to school, even if it's just half days, your child care costs will drop significantly. At the same time, a stay-at-home parent might be considering a return to work. You might decide to look for a job with hours that allow you to still be home for school drop-offs and pickups, or perhaps you will work full-time and rely on before and after school child care for a few hours a day. As your children become more independent, the stay-at-home parent could also consider a part-time job while the working parent holds down the fort those evenings or weekends.

Recommended Reading

If you give your child too much; too many toys, not enough rules, too many activities—you run the risk of overindulging them. You can see problems in an overindulged toddler immediately—they are manifest in tantrums, moodiness, and unwillingness to listen. Actually, that's how all toddlers act at some point! But it isn't how they should act all the time, and particularly not into their teenager years and beyond. So how does overindulgence in childhood impact an individual in adulthood? The authors of **How Much Is Enough? Everything You Need to Know to Steer Clear of Overindulgence and Raise Likeable, Responsible, and Respectful Children** *by Jean Illsley Clarke, Connie Dawson, and David Bredehoft claim that overindulged toddlers turn into teens and adults who lack even the most basic life management skills, morals and emotions. The authors provide advice on how to prevent or reverse this sort of damage. Best of all, there's even advice on how to deal with well-meaning friends and family, including grandparents, who overindulge your children. For additional information,* **The Millionaire Next Door** *by Thomas J. Stanley and William D. Danko dedicated a whole chapter to what they call economic outpatient care, where parents provide adult children with financial support and end up undermining their children's capacity to become financially competent and independant.*

Finding Full-Time Child Care

There are three basic types of full-time child care services: informal care, formal care, and live-in or live-out care. Choosing which care option is best for you and your family means figuring out the pros and cons of each.

Many parents choose informal, privately arranged types of care either within their own home or at the home of caregivers, such as those of grandparents and other relatives or friends. This option is usually the least costly and provides the greatest flexibility.

Formal care is offered by child care or daycare centres, nursery schools, and family-based daycares (also known as dayhomes). Unlike informal care, these programs are subject to provincial and territorial regulations and may be inspected and monitored. Daycares are generally facilities in commercial buildings, strip malls, offices or renovated houses. The staff at these facilities often have specific training or certification, their facility is likely very clean and well stocked with toys, books, and safe sleeping arrangements, and they generally provide all snacks and meals. Some daycares have earlier drop-off and later pickup times than family-based daycares. One disadvantage of formal care is that with the larger number of children in one facility, your child could be exposed to a lot more colds, sniffles, and flus than if they were in a smaller group.

Like daycares, family-based daycares have their advantages and disadvantages. They are generally a few hundred dollars a month less than formal daycares, may provide drop-off and pickup service to locals schools or preschools, and are run by one consistent caregiver with whom you may develop a good friendship. Many family-based daycares providers care for their own children in addition to a government determined maximum of other children. Depending on the provider, you may even find one with a set daily schedule that includes crafts, storytime, and learning-based outings, much like a daycare.

The biggest disadvantage I've found with family-based daycares was in handling the sometimes impromptu time off the operator needed. If she or her children were sick, I would have to find alternate care. I would also be forced to plan my vacation schedule around hers, or again, find alternate care. Both my husband and I don't have the kind of employment where you can simply call in and take a sick day at the eleventh hour, so last minute closures at a dayhome were nightmares for us. As a result, we began to research live-in caregivers.

Live-in and live-out caregivers work in your own home. Though this can be the priciest option, it's the one that offers the most flexibility. These caregivers usually handle light household chores, and may prepare in part or in whole the evening meal. Live-out caregivers are the most expensive option, as you'll need to pay them minimum wage or more, and you aren't able to deduct expenses for room and board. When you employ a caregiver (or nanny), Canada Revenue Agency considers you as an employer and you both must deduct and pay taxes—try and dodge this by claiming the caregiver is an independent contractor and you could get penalized with big fines by Canada Revenue Agency.

If you're interested in hiring a live-in caregiver, the Canadian government offers a live-in caregiver program in which the caregiver must reside at your home—the one in which they work. There are rules outlining how to apply for the program (for both the employer and caregiver) and rules governing hours of work, pay, and salary deductions for room and board. Caregivers do require their own room in your home, and preferably a private bathroom for their exclusive use as well.

There are benefits to both employer and caregiver. The majority of caregivers who apply to come work and in Canada are women—usually mothers themselves with small children of their own back home—who are using the program as a stepping stone to becoming permanent residents, so they are eventually able to bring over their own family to start a new life in Canada.

When I was pregnant with our second child and my consignment store was still requiring a lot of my day-to-day attention, we decided to hire a live-in caregiver. Immediately we knew we had made the right decision for us. While it was more expensive than the previous child care arrangements we had, it was 100% reliable. When the girls developed croup one after the other for three weeks in a row, we were still able to head to work, at least after the worst days were over, knowing the girls were being well cared for in their own home. Genny was a huge help with the cooking, cleaning, and laundry, giving us more time to enjoy the kids in the evenings and weekends instead of spending much of our time dealing with mundane household tasks. When our third child came along, I had the extra help I desperately needed, and the cost more or less equated with what I would have paid for out-of-home care anyway. Best of all, on days when we both had to work late, there was no mad scramble to make a pick-up time at a daycare. On freezing mornings, we didn't have to bundle children into a cold car at 7:00 am. This type of care has disadvantages too. You may find a live-in caregiver is too intrusive upon your personal time or space. Many are unable to drive and, if they don't create strong local networks of friends, your children may not have day time playdates.

Whether you're going the daycare, family-based daycare, or live-in/live-out caregiver route, you should give yourself plenty of time to find the right arrangement, and sign up on any necessary waitlists. After a few bad experiences with unreliable family-based daycare, I tried to find a daycare that could accommodate both my children when I planned to return to shift work at the store. With only a few daycares in my small city to choose from, I was looking at waiting lists in excess of two years! The process we had to go through in order to bring over a live-in caregiver from another country took us nine months, though it can be accomplished more quickly if you find a caregiver already in Canada who is looking for a new position.

Grandma, Grandpa, Babysitter?

As a generation of adults delay becoming parents until their thirties or later, it's becoming increasingly likely that the children's grandparents may be retired or semi-retired. In many families, it's these grandparents who are being asked to provide care for the babies beyond the occasional Friday night out.

This type of informal care is usually the least costly arrangement for parents returning to work. In some families, this care is provided free. In her book, *Wonderful Ways To Love a Grandchild*, Judy Ford recommends that grandparents take the initiative in setting guidelines around occasional care. "Let your children know in advance about whether you have other plans, or just want to be by yourselves at certain times. This gives the parents ample time to make other arrangements. Be honest about how much babysitting you are willing to do. Babysitting when you don't want to only creates tensions between you and your adult children," she says.

Julie turned to her parents for help with the care of her 20-month-old daughter, Kalynah. "My dad is retired and my mom is still working. They offered to watch her when Mike and I are busy with work." Grandparents Howard and Annie are thrilled with the arrangement. "I love children and Kalynah is my first granddaughter." Annie adds that they enjoy helping, "because we know how hard working our daughter and son-in-law are." It's important that all parties involved have an open and honest discussion about the terms of the care, including how often and where care will be provided, what amount of notice of any change in plans is required, and what remuneration, if any, will be provided, if any. Parents should also be sure to discuss with the grandparents specific details about care, especially concerning issues that have changed over the last few decades, such as feeding and safety.

Julie has experienced some concerns over choices her parents make, but they've been relatively minor. "My parents say Kalynah's not wearing enough even though she has four layers on, but I think she's too hot because she's whining." The family has the added bonus of having the grandparents available to babysit. Kalynah is half Caucasian and half Chinese, and the caregiving grandparents are teaching her their language and heritage. "We hope that as she grows older, she'll embrace her Chinese heritage," says Howard.

Though Howard and Annie aren't paid specifically for their time, Julie does ensure she gives them a lump sum of money each month to cover expenses such as diapers, milk, and clothes.

Whether the grandparents will accept payment or not, it's still important to thank them in a non-monetary way for their generosity. Bonnie has taken her parents out for dinner in appreciation for caring for her three children, aged six, two and five months. "I've also bought my mom the odd item she's wanted, such as a purse, or perfume," says Bonnie. A gift can be expensive, such as tickets to a concert or a day at the spa, or it can inexpensive—a thoughtful card with a heartfelt message, or a used copy of a book you think they'd like, with a personal inscription.

Getting Schooled

These days, school isn't the free babysitter it used to be! Even at public schools, school fees, mandatory fundraisers and the back-to-school shopping hype can all send your expenses skyrocketing in August and September. Here's a look at what's involved when it comes to classroom costs.

Private Education

We all want the best for our children, but does that necessarily mean we have to enrol them in the very best schools, regardless of the costs? Each year, the independent research organization, The Fraser Institute, releases a report that grades schools in each province and identifies which are among the best. But when the top institutions all happen to be those whose pupils come from higher income households where income levels is many times higher than the household income of students attending the lowest ranking schools, frankly, the report says more about socio-economic disparities than teaching ability. Some parents choose private schools for religious reasons or to maintain a family tradition rather than some other specifically educational rationale.

Private school tuition can range anywhere from $6,000 to as much as $20,000 a year a more. The average annual household income of the families who send their children to the top private schools in Calgary is more than $300,000. If sending your child to a private school will be a major financial sacrifice to your household, consider what sacrifices your child might make as well. While they may be presented with every opportunity for a top-notch education, if they suffer from low self esteem because they aren't privy to the same weekend experiences as their peers, can't wear the same clothes, or drive the same car, how will this affect their overall childhood and teenage experience?

If private school is a priority for your family and you're not earning $300,000 a year (and if you're reading this book, I suspect you're not!) you may still be able to work it into your budget with the help of scholarships, financial aid, or interest-free loans. You can contact the schools you're considering to talk about payment options with them; while their average family is very well off, they are used to accommodating families in different circumstances as well.

Back to School

Didn't they just get out of school a few weeks ago? Before you know it, you're reviewing school supply lists, looking at last year's ratty backpack, and figuring out if they have any pants that are in god shape. Probably the worst thing you can do when back-to-school shopping is blindly head to the nearest mall with your wallet at hand. Your child, whether 6 or 16, will likely not understand why they can't have that one pair of just-right jeans that would max out your entire clothing budget if you have that conversion in the middle of a clothing store. So here are a few tips to help keep your budget in line while back-to-school shopping.

- Did the closet fairy steal all your kids clothing the night before back-to-school shopping? No! So you don't need to replace every item in their wardrobe. Before you leave the house, have a discussion with your child about what they really need—how many pairs of pants, hoodies, shoes, etc.? T-shirts that still fit can add warmth by layering over long sleeved shirts. Dresses become tunics with capri tights.
- Set a budget for each child. If your child is older and has savings of their own, this is a great time to introduce the concept of topping up. If you're willing to pay $60 for sneakers and the ones they covet are $110, they can consider paying the difference out of their own savings.
- Don't buy everything at once! Many a parent has experienced a child come home in a state after the first week of school because their clothing was all wrong. By spending part of your budget before school starts, and part after, you'll ensure you still have money left for that specific pair of jeans or the shirt your child still wants.
- Set aside some money for snagging great deals on next year's summer clothing. In your haste to find long sleeved shirts and cords, don't forget to check out clearance racks for bargain basement priced swim and summer wear for next year.
- For older children and teens, it's time to talk quality. Do you want to spend $15 on a cheap backpack that rips before the end of the year, or invest $35 in a higher quality one that will see them off to university? I still use my hiking backpack which I had when I graduated from high school 14 years ago. Sometimes the higher price tag is worth it.

- When it comes to supplies, check flyers for the loss leaders—the packs of crayons, paper, binders and school bags sold at deep discounts and often below cost just to get you through the door. Don't hesitate to pick up more than you'll need for the first day of school—if you need to replenish supplies in January, those super sale prices will be long gone.

School Fees and Fundraisers

Public schools are supposed to be free—courtesy of our municipal property taxes of course. Yet school fees are increasing every year in many districts. You might be asked to pay basic enrolment fees, extra charges for field trips, mandatory school supply packages, lunch program fees, and busing costs. Later on you'll be expected to help out with fundraising—hustling overpriced wrapping paper or chocolate bars, or ordering from book catalogues and attending silent auction events for which you're expected to secure a donation.

In British Columbia, lawsuits exist or are in the process of being filed against various school districts, in which it is claimed that by charging fees, the school districts are in violation of the British Columbia School Act. Many provincial school acts outline exactly what schools can collect fees for, but some school districts make it difficult for parents to determine if they are being fairly billed, or if their school district is charging fees for items not permitted under their provincial school act. If you have questions about the fees you're being charged, start by talking to the principal of the school.

You may be able to find your school fees published online, or you can call your child's school to ask for a breakdown of the coming year's school fees. Knowing in advance what you'll have to shell out for each child will allow you to save on a monthly basis a proportion of those anticipated school-related costs in a separate account, so you're neither surprised or burdened with the whole cost in September. If you think you might qualify, ask about reduced school fees for low-income families, and donated school supply programs or breakfast and lunch programs.

Get a Haircut, and Get a Real Job

When your children are old enough, you can introduce the idea of a part-time job and earning extra money for the items they covet that either lie beyond the means of your family budget, or you simply do not want to spend money on. For one-time purchases they could do tasks for neighbours, or take on a newspaper flyer route, shovel snow, run errands for a family member or neighbour, or find any number of cash-earning tasks locally.

Eventually, a part-time job will be a possibility. Studies have shown that a part-time job of less than 15 hours a week does not have a detrimental effect upon schoolwork. However, if your child is playing competitive hockey six nights a week, or is struggling academically, adding a job to their weekly schedule could be asking too much.

There are so many benefits to having your child take on the responsibility of a part-time job, regardless of your income and ability to pay for all the various things they want. They'll be accountable in a new way, with the responsibility of learning new tasks, performing them adequately, working with people in various age groups and in different socio-economic circumstances.

If your children have their own source of income, you can bet it will have a positive impact on your family budget. Unless they're saving 100% of it for their future post-secondary education, it's time to set the expectation that their own money must now be used for anything above and beyond the basics. It's not just for the sake of your own budget that you should introduce this plan towards shared responsibility, but for their own future as well.

Many teenagers live the high life at home during high school, and even throughout the duration of their post-secondary education, with little to no real idea that they've got it so good. If mom and dad have been shelling out to pay for car insurance, hair appointments and designer clothing while their princess is still a student, how will she ever learn to accept the lower standard of living she'll be forced into when she moves out? If each child spends $20,000 of mom and dad's money a year, when they move out the additional $15,000 a year they'll require for rent and food will mean they have an after-tax spending habit of $35,000 per year. Will their very first job pay them the $55,000 a year they'll need to maintain the lifestyle to which they've become accustomed? Unlikely! But what a shock for the indulged twenty-something who now believes they "deserve" to go snowboarding every weekend, the latest fashions regardless of the price, and the closet full of designer duds they already own.

If you're not teaching your children to differentiate between *needs* and *wants*, budgeting and saving, then who will? It'll be impossible to teach them once they've left the nest, and getting the message through before they've developed a deeply entrenched habit and history of entitlement is vital to their future financial independence.

The Costs of Camps and Classes

I overhead a mom talking to a friend about the number of classes her daughter was enrolled in this spring. "Lauren is taking dance on Saturday mornings before her music class, then ringette practices once a week, and her skating class is weekly too. I don't put her in anything else on Tuesdays and Thursdays though—she's just too tired from preschool." Yup, preschool plus four separate activities a week, for a child not yet old enough to write her own name!

I've never really understood the reason for putting my kids into every available activity. For younger children it can cost hundreds of dollars a month, for older kids, such as those enrolled in competitive hockey or dance, it can literally be thousands. You end up ferrying your child to class after class after class, with no time built in for lazy Saturday mornings making waffles with dad, and they might miss out on family events, birthday parties and more. It's great to have kids involved in something, but do they need to be in everything? Why do they have to take music, art, dance, gymnastics, hockey *and* soccer?

Parents should take a step back and think about how each activity will affect their family as a whole before blindly lining up with chequebook in hand to sign up for everything under the sun. What activities is your child really interested in? Which ones are their friends in? Are there community classes that do just as good a job as private classes for half the price? Could you spread the activities out over the year, so they're not in everything all the time, or are they ready to choose just one to focus on?

For some community recreation organizations, even those whose programs are run as private businesses, there is often a volunteer or fundraising component to the activity too. Are you going to have to ferry your kids around your neighbourhood supporting a bottle drive on a rare no-game Sunday? Will you have to pester colleagues for cash for overpriced gift wrap, chocolate bars, or cookie dough? Remember that fundraising is a two-way street—if you're asking for cash for popcorn, you'd better be willing to shell out when your co-worker's kid comes by selling magazine subscriptions.

When it comes to camps, there may be fewer options in a variety of price points. Do some checking around—your church or community group may run day or weeklong camps at more affordable rates than the privately run camps. If you have a few willing friends, you could create your own day camp program for a week or more. Each parent takes responsibility for one day of the week and organizes games, crafts, and fun outdoor activities around a theme, such as pirates, super heroes, dinosaurs, or more. A $20 investment, a few hours of planning, and one day of leading the camp earns you four kid-free days plus a huge savings over the registration cost of a more structured day camp.

What About Fluffy and Fido?

What kid hasn't begged their mom and dad for a puppy, a kitty, or a fish? You know they'll be a lot of work, and though your kids promise they'll take care of their new pet, you know who'll end up scooping poop at 6:00 am and trying to fit in a walk for the dog before you head to bed. Then there's the expense!

We had a cat long before kids, and he cost us about $65 a month, after food, litter, and veterinary bills were taken into account. So we knew pet ownership was a large expense. For some reason we decided one of our friend's black Labrador puppies would be a great new companion for our kids. After spending $600 on veterinary bills for her shots and to have her spayed, $200 on a bed, crate, bowls and various dog toys (the larger items bought used), $60 a month on food, and $250 on training, we ended up finding her a new home before the year was up. So much for a free puppy! We just didn't have the patience to wait until she grew out of the destructive and over-exuberant puppy stage, or the time to devote to walking and training her. It was a very expensive lesson to learn. And we didn't even have to deal with the inevitable extra costs of illness or injury.

It was a difficult situation when Joelene's beloved bull mastiff Maggie required the replacement of her left knee. The veterinary bill for the operation was just over $4200 with another $180 for the radiograph that she required eight weeks later. "Maggie's surgery definitely took a toll on our savings," says Joelene. "When I revamped our budget, we had to cut back on other items that we didn't necessarily need, for example, cutting back on eating out, doggie daycare, hobby funds, and the money that we allocated for bank withdrawls. It will take some time of sticking with this reduced budget to get us back up to the amount we were at before we withdrew funds for Maggie's surgery. However I would do it all again in a heartbeat, because she's like one of our children."

If you think you can afford it and your family can handle the responsibility a pet represents, visit your local animal shelter. There you can talk to a volunteer about the full costs of owning the pet you're thinking of adopting and/or buying. If it's $75 a month, it would be a good idea to save that money every month for the next year in a separate bank account. You'll be certain you can afford the animal, and you'll now have an emergency fund saved in case your pet gets sick and needs special medical care. Speaking of medical care, if you live in a big city, investigate the rural areas surrounding you for less expensive veterinary services. A thirty-minute drive saved my mother hundreds of dollars when her golden retriever needed medical attention.

If you still want to add a furry companion to your family, consider re-homing a pet that turned out not to be the right fit with its current owners, going to an animal shelter, or contacing a breeder. Purchasing a dog from a pet shop may get you a puppy mill puppy, and the mixed-breeds-no-papers pooches they sell are generally more expensive than a purebred dog from a reliable breeder.

Finally, remember that everything new gets old, and kids lose interest very quickly, even in kittens and puppies. One week they're obsessed with the hamster, the next they've forgotten they even had one.

Thinking about pet insurance? You might want to think twice. Read the fine print of any policy you're considering—some policies will cap payouts and you'll end up paying more in premiums that you will ever claim in coverage. Other policies are so restrictive that your pet's needs may never be covered. Pet insurance is basically a euphemism for enforced savings—something you can do on your own, and earn investment interest too, if you're committed to the task.

Recommended Surfing

- *Frugal for Life* <**www.frugalforlife.blogspot. com**>
- *Savings* <**www.frugal.families.com/blog**>
- *The Save Money Blog* <**www.savemoneyblog. net**>

Final Thought

If you thought the unspoken pressure from other moms to have the best stroller was tough—living with a preteen who acts as though they will suffer immediate social death if they don't have a fourteenth video game is really tough. Trying to save money when hockey fees are due, your kids have grown out of the gear you just bought and the schedule seems to make dinners at home impossible is agony! I hope you've realized that it's not a lost cause, and you can still save money and make your family budget work even as your kids grow. If you've read this book when your children are young, you now know why it's so important not to go overboard in your spending on stuff before baby can talk—that cash will come in handy when you're faced with deciding whether or not you can afford sports, tutoring, or vacations with those that require paid seats!

CHAPTER ELEVEN

Not According to Plan

LIFE HAS A WAY OF disrupting the best laid plans. Have you thought about how you'll handle the financial implications of fertility problems, finding out you're having multiples, raising a disabled child, or separation or divorce? This chapter deals with some of the more challenging special situations some parents face.

Fertility Facts

If you've ever participated in the high school sex education ritual of "caring" for an egg or baby doll to learn the responsibility involved in caring for a baby, you probably had it drilled into your head that unprotected sex equals baby! Unfortunately, as many couples learn, getting pregnant isn't as easy as leaving the condoms in the bedside drawer for just one night.

A normal fertile couple has about a one in five chance of achieving pregnancy in any given month of unprotected sex. In theory, 85% to 90% of women attempting to become pregnant can expect to conceive during the first year. Some couples view this time before getting pregnant as part of the mental preparation time they need to get ready for the arrival of the baby—others find it excruciating to discover each month that they still haven't been successful.

> It took me a year to get pregnant the first time. I had given up the second time after five years, deciding that it was my fate not to have a second child. I remember going to tea with a friend of mine and telling her I had given up and resolved myself to the fact that I had been blessed with one child. That night I found out I was pregnant again! Nothing can

help with the prospect of not being able to conceive except to continue living life fully and enjoy what you do have, not what you don't. The support of my husband and friends are what made things better.

Susan, mom of two

What if you've been trying for months and nothing's happening? You may have fertility problems. From a scientific point of view, infertility is the diminished or absent capacity to produce offspring. It does not mean that you are sterile, or will never be able to produce children. Many couples find that they are in fact fertile, but they've simply been miscalculating the fertility window, which is quite short. A woman is most fertile during ovulation and one to two days before ovulation. As soon as you make the decision to start trying to get pregnant, book an appointment with your doctor. They'll ask you a number of questions about your medical history as it relates to fertility. They may also encourage you to track your menstrual cycles. If you do have a problem conceiving, this record will prove helpful.

Recommended Reading

Taking Charge of Your Fertility by Toni Weschler is a massive tome that covers everything you could possibly want to know about fertility awareness. Her book is a must-read for anyone having difficulty conceiving.

If you're under 30, you'll probably need to try for at least a year before your doctor will order fertility tests. If you're older, you may be encouraged to go for testing earlier. You may also be referred for testing if you've had a history of problems with your menstrual cycle or have had miscarriages or pelvic inflammatory disease.

Infertility testing is covered by provincial health care programs. However, you must receive referrals to special clinics or doctors, and wait times for appointments can be many months.

When You've Waited Long Enough—Fertility Treatment

As Canadians, we are extremely lucky to have a health care system that offers prenatal and labour care free of charge. While you're stocking up on diapers and outfitting the nursery, you don't need to also fill out loan applications for the delivery fees. In contrast, an American mother without insurance can expect to pay as much as $10,000 for a routine birth in a hospital. However, to take advantage of the Canadian system, you need to get pregnant first, and that comes with a hefty price tag if it doesn't come naturally. If you've been diagnosed as requiring assisted reproductive technology (ART) to become pregnant, the costs involved are high, the stress immeasurable, and the outcome uncertain. There are a number of treatments available, with varying success rates, risks, and fees.

Polycystic ovarian syndrome (PCOS) is a common cause of infertility in women. Women with this syndrome do not ovulate (release eggs) regularly and therefore have irregular menstrual cycles. Their ovaries contain multiple small cystic structures that give the ovaries a characteristic "polycystic" (many cysts) appearance using ultrasound. The least expensive treatment, and least effective, is the drug clomiphene (sometimes called by its trade name Clomid), used alone or in conjunction with Intrauterine Insemination (IUI). Clomiphene increases the woman's follicle stimulating hormone (FSH) at the beginning of her cycle with the intention of providing the ovulation of two follicles (eggs) and to improve follicular hormonal production. IUI can be performed at the time of ovulation to increase the chances of pregnancy. As there are reports of increased risk of ovarian cancer after 12 cycles of treatment, its use is often restricted to three or four cycles. However, this correlation has recently been challenged. There is also a decreased chance of pregnancy after each cycle of clomiphene administration. The cost for a clomiphene and IUI cycle is between $200 to $300 and the pregnancy rate is approximately 5% per cycle. A more recent method for treating ovulation problems in women with PCOS is to use metformin (brand name Glucophage) with or without clomiphene.

Another option is superovulation combined with IUI. This involves daily injections meant to override the normal natural single egg selection of the ovary and stimulate to maturity two to four eggs. Once the eggs are ready, a woman will receive an injection of human chorionic gonadotropin (HCG) to ovulate the eggs and will have an intrauterine insemination the following day. The success rate of this treatment leading to a pregnancy is 10% to 12% per cycle. The drugs required cost between $1,500 and $2,500, with a clinical fee of around $350. Attempts are generally limited to no more than six cycles.

Finally, in vitro fertilization (IVF) is the most effective and most expensive treatment. IVF is often used when a woman's fallopian tubes are blocked or when a man's sperm count is low. The ovaries are stimulated using drugs to produce multiple eggs, which are removed when mature. The mature eggs are fertilized with the man's semen in a culture dish, hence the dated term "test tube baby." Fertilized eggs (embryos) are then implanted directly in the woman's uterus. Pregnancy rates for this procedure vary between 25% and 44% per cycle.

In Ontario, IVF was provided for free until 1992. Today, IVF is available and publicly funded only when a woman has dual blocked fallopian tubes. In such cases, three attempts are covered by health care. In 2002, Quebec established a 30% refundable tax credit for IVF treatment. Residents of Quebec may also be entitled to a refundable tax credit for expenses related to fertility treatment. You may also be able to claim your travel costs. For specific information, visit the Canada Revenue Agency website at <**www. cra-arc.gc.ca**>. Few other provinces offer any financial assistance.

One cycle of IVF can cost between $4,500 and $6,500, with additional drug costs of at least $1,500 or more per cycle of treatment. One mom I know spent more than $6,000 on the drug component alone. Usually, more than one cycle of treatment is necessary. On average, IVF will cost about $16,000 to achieve a successful pregnancy. This consists of three cycles and the necessary medications. Older women requiring more doses of fertility drugs, or additional procedures including egg or sperm donation, embryo freezing, storage and subsequent transfer will find the costs to be even higher. Finally, if you don't live in a city that provide fertility clinic services, you may have to drive for many hours to your multiple clinic appointments, or even relocate to another city for a each treatment cycle, relying on hotels and restaurant food for an indeterminate period of time. Travel, accommodation and food costs increase the overall cost of treatment.

Very few private insurance companies cover the cost of this sort of treatment and/or the fertility drugs. In online bulletin boards, hopeful parents post requests for the names of these companies with the intention of applying for jobs with employers providing this coverage. If you're not certain that you have coverage through your employer, request the policy in writing, and ask to have any unclear clauses further defined and clarified in writing.

If applicable to your financial situation, check with your local health region to see if there are any groups that may offer assistance with fertility treatment costs.

> Our twins are IVF babies. We drained our savings account that we were planning on using to buy our first home to undergo fertility treatments. We don't regret it for a minute. It has set us back a few years on purchasing our home, but we do have our own home now and are glad we went this route.
>
> *Jennifer, mom of two*

The Adoption Option

It isn't just married couples with fertility problems who turn to adoption. Though some adoption agencies have certain restrictions, for the most part, any Canadian citizen over the age of eighteen without a criminal record can adopt a child. Those eligible for consideration as adoptive parents include single parents, gay couples, and couples who already have biological children.

Adoption is a provincial matter and, as such, the rules for adoption vary from province to province. As these laws change constantly, it is important to ensure you are up-to-date with the regulations for your province, which can usually be found on your provincial government's website.

There are three main choices in adoption: public domestic, private domestic, and international (from the United States and overseas). The option you choose may be based on the costs involved, waiting times, and the type of child you would like to add to your family.

The process of adopting a child doesn't happen overnight. Depending on the choices you make, the process can have wildly divergent timelines for completion. If you're seeking a Caucasian newborn with no known health problems, you'll likely wait for many years. However, if you are interested in adopting an older child, perhaps with identified developmental disabilities, you may need to wait only a few months.

> Although I understand how different things are from a parent's perspective, as a child who was adopted by my dad at the age of eight, I can honestly say that I didn't care how I had come to be. What I cared about was that I had someone to love and call my "dad". As a child, someone committing that they will love you forever by adopting you is the greatest gift you can ever receive.
>
> *Nicole, mom of two*

Public Adoptions

Arranged through government agencies, public adoptions are free, but the children available for adoption are often children with behavioural or learning disabilities, sibling groups, or other children who for one reason or another are difficult to place. The waiting period for a healthy newborn can be nearly a decade, while the waiting period for a higher-needs child is relatively short.

Private Domestic Adoptions

Adopting a child through the private system is desirable to many parents because they have access to healthy newborns after much shorter waiting periods (usually less than three years). The costs start at about $6,000 and can be as much as $15,000 or more. For many parents, these costs are offset by the benefit—potentially shorter waiting times. The waiting period depends on the availability of children, and whether you're conducting the search on your own, or using a provincially-approved licensee or agency. It also depends on how long it takes for the birth mother or birth family to choose your family. Other families just signing up to receive a child may receive one before families who have been waiting for years. If you have not been selected in a year, you may be required to pay for a home study update. In some provinces there are licensed agencies you can use to assist your search or simply to help make adoptive parent profile more available to birth mothers.

There are also legal fees to consider. In private domestic adoptions the birth mother may change her mind and keep her baby, but you will still have to pay the legal fees involved specific to this failed adoption.

International Adoption (including United States)

About 1,500 to 2,000 babies are adopted each year through international adoptions. This is the most popular method of adoption, despite the high costs and mountains of red tape. These adoptions can have shorter waiting periods (often less than two years), but the price tag is steep— between $20,000 and $35,000.

Interested parents will first select the country from which they wish to adopt a child, and then select other factors such as preferred age, gender, and race. They'll then work with a private agency to navigate complicated provincial adoption law, immigration law, and the regulations of the child's country of origin. International adoptions are a good place for non-traditional couples to find a child. It's important to note that all international adoptions are of children older than six months and, as with any adoptions, good health is impossible to guarantee.

Special Needs Adoption

Special needs children are understandably more difficult to place, but arguably they are the children who might benefit the most from a loving home. If you're prepared to adopt a special needs child, you can do so quickly and relatively easily at little or no cost. However, it takes an incredible individual or couple to assume this sort of responsibility. These children may have been neglected, abused or abandoned. They may have deep and long-lasting emotional, mental, or physical problems that can impact their ability to function normally in your family and in society in general. Yet these problems can be overcome, and many government resources are available to support you if you choose this route.

Foster Care

Foster care is required when children are temporarily removed from their natural home and family and placed in the care of people with whom they have no previous relationship. Generally speaking, when provincial authorities move in and apprehend children from a dangerous or perceived as potentially dangerous domestic situation, the children are placed in foster care under a temporary guardianship order. Foster care arrangements might last for a few days, weeks, months or years, depending on the precise circumstances for apprehension. Though the arrangements vary from province to province, foster parents generally receive training, support and compensation for the care they provide to foster children.

Many provinces have also formalised Foster-to-Adopt programs where foster parents may be placed with a baby or child whom the foster parents might eventually adopt if long term temporary guardianship becomes permanent. While fostering an infant with the hopes of adoption could potentially be more emotionally fraught with ups and downs through the process, it can often be a faster route to adoption than simply waiting to be chosen by a birth mother.

Recommended Surfing

The Adoption Council of Canada (ACC) is the umbrella organization for adoption in Canada. Their website, <www.adoption.ca>, is a source of much information about adoption in Canada, as well as providing links to provincial websites where you will find the most up-to-date information for your home jurisdiction.

The More, The Merrier

If you've been blessed with multiples, your expenses won't necessarily be double or triple the expenses of the parents of a single child. You might decide to buy two of certain items, like swings or cribs, but when it comes to vibrating chairs or play mats, your multiples will get their first lesson in taking turns!

If you discover you're expecting more than one baby, your first stop should be Multiple Births Canada's website at <**www.multiplebirths canada.org**>. Multiple Births Canada is a national support organization for multiple birth families and individuals in Canada. Members receive discounts for various products and have access to support networks for people in special situations. This website has a list of affiliated organizations at the local level, but not all multiple birth clubs in Canada are affiliated with the group. It's worth doing a web search to find out if your city has a twins and triplets, or multiple births club. If your local club has an annual sale, generally members will get first dibs on hitting the sale—and this can be a great bonus.

Raising a Special Needs Child

Whether you've adopted or given birth to a special needs child, the road ahead will be incredibly challenging but rewarding as well. There are a variety of federal and provincial programs available to assist families with the often high medical costs often associated with raising a special needs child, and many community organizations have programs in place to help as well. You should be able to get in touch with the right organizations with help from your local community health organization or hospital.

If you have a special needs child, what will happen to your child when you and your spouse are no longer able to care for them? The Registered Disability Savings Plan (RDSP) allows people with disabilities (or their friends or family members) to put money aside in an account where it will grow tax free until it is needed. There is a $200,000 lifetime contribution limit but no annual limits on contributions. In conjunction with the savings plan, the government offers a Canada Disability Savings Grant. For families with an annual net income of less than $75,769 the grant will contribute $3 for every $1 contributed on the first $500 saved, and $2 for every $1 contributed on the next $1,000. For families with net income over $75,769, the grant is $1 for every $1 contributed up to $1,000. In addition, for low income families, the Canada Disability Savings Bond provides an annual $1,000 grant without any contributions required, with a limit of $20,000 over your lifetime.

Is it Over?

Unfortunately, despite the best of intentions, relationships change. Even the arrival of children can have a negative impact on a relationship—highlighting one partner's unwillingness to share in household duties or fundamental differences in parenting philosophies, adding to overwhelming financial stresses or other disparities between partners. Your happily-ever-after plan might change of your own accord, or you could be hit with an unexpected illness, disability, or even death. Have you thought about what will happen to your family if one of you were injured and could no longer work? How would you survive an extended period of unemployment? What if your spouse decided they wanted out of the relationship and wanted joint custody of the kids—or worse, suddenly wanted nothing to do with the children?

Expect the Best, Prepare for the Worst

We talked about life and disability insurance in Chapter Five, and I hope it convinced you to put down this book and call an insurance agent immediately.

There is a CPP disability benefit available to people who have contributed enough to the CPP, and whose disability prevents them from working at any job on a regular basis over an extended period of time, or if the disability is likely to result in death. In March of 2009, the average monthly payment from the CPP disability benefit for a qualifying disabled person was $816.81, with a maximum of $1,105.99. Assuming you qualified for the program, would this be enough to replace your income or that of your spouse if one of you were to become disabled? There are also benefits available to the children of a person who receives a CPP disability benefit—in 2009, this amount was $213.99 monthly per child.

In the event of your partner's death, there are a number of steps to take even amidst the preparations for a funeral, wake or memorial service. First, contact the human resourced department at your recently decreased partner's place of employment. You should receive a final cheque that includes any outstanding bonuses or vacation pay. If you don't already know what death benefits you'll be entitled to receive, now's the time to ask. Your partner's employer may have a small life insurance pay-out, pension benefit pay-outs, or continuation of health benefits for surviving family members, all of which you will need to understand.

You'll also want to review the Canada Pension Plan program for contributors. CPP survivor benefits are paid to a deceased contributor's estate, surviving spouse, or common-law partner and dependent children. The death benefit is a one time payment to, or on behalf of, the estate of a deceased Canada Pension Plan contributor. The survivor's pension is a monthly pension paid to the surviving spouse or common-law partner of a deceased contributor. The children's benefit is a monthly benefit for dependent children of a deceased contributor.

You must apply for these benefits—they will not be sent automatically and, if you wait too long, you may lose that eligibility. Application kits are available from any Human Resources and Skills Development Canada Centre and most funeral homes. The amount you'll receive depends on how much and for how long the deceased contributed to the CPP. The amount a surviving spouse or common-law partner will receive depends on whether the spouse or common-law partner is also receiving a CPP disability or retirement pension. The calculations to determine exactly how much you would receive are available online at <**www.rhdcc-hrsdc.gc.ca/eng/isp/ cpp/survivor.shtml**>, but they're challenging to understand. It might be helpful to know that in 2009, the average survivor's pension on behalf of the deceased partner was $366.90 per month.

Infidelity and Domestic Violence

One point I've been trying to get across in this book is this: as parents, being less judgmental is a good goal to which we should all aspire. We succeed in setting a good example for our children, it invariably results in our being more compassionate towards others.

At a recent girl's-only dinner, the conversation turned to the topic of cheating spouses. A single girlfriend commented that no one should ever stay with a spouse who cheated. She felt the partner who stayed with a partner who strayed had no self-esteem, or were "stupid". I strongly disagreed. First, many women (or men) are honestly shocked by confessions of their partner's infidelity, as are other family members confided in. The infidelity could be a symptom of a larger problem in the marriage that can be successfully resolved, with or without counselling and support. Or it could be a deal breaker.

It's even more complicated when children are involved, especially in lower or single income families. Leave him? Sounds easy, but it's not. She'll pack her two children under five in the car and go. Find a cheap rental apartment in a seedy neighbourhood. Switch the kids to a new school. If her husband is angry and abusive, he might not pay support, and she'll be too afraid to fight him for it. If she hasn't worked in years, the best she might be able to find is an entry-level secretarial job. One pay cheque pays the rent, the other child care. So she considers going on welfare, because at least then she'll be back home with her kids, not riding the bus with them to daycare at 7:30 am and getting them home at 6:30 pm. But what about her self-esteem? What example is she setting for her children? Yet if she stays, how will their lives be impacted?

You can see how the standard, indignant advice to "leave him" isn't as easy as it sounds. There are significant ramifications to both staying or leaving, emotionally and financially.

If you are facing difficulties in your marriage, being proactive and seeking help before the problems reach epic proportions is wise. You may have an employee assistance program that could cover some or all of the costs of counselling, and many community programs are available that offer support and counselling to couples on the brink as well. If a separation, divorce, or perhaps even escape is critical, government programs do exist—often even in small communities—that can help you to make the changes you need to make for your family, and get safely settled somewhere else. If you're not sure where to start looking, visit your doctor's office or community resource centre—they'll have information on all of the services available to you locally.

Final Thought

If the worst happened, would you be ready? How would cataclysmic changes in your relationship or life affect your ability to provide for your kids? If you don't have the answers to these questions, you need to make a plan and act on it now, whether it be writing up a will or investigating life and disability insurance. While you may think you can't afford to right now, you simply can't afford not to.

In Closing

Children aren't born with a price tag. You can buy them all of the things they need brand new, only buy used, or a combination of the two. You can send them to private school or utilize the public system. Give in to the "gimmies", or teach them the value of money. The impact your children have on your finances is entirely up to you. Whether you've created a mountain of debt because you've never examined your options carefully when it came to your spending, saving and credit habits, or have been teetering on the edge of falling behind, now's the time to take what you've learned in this book and step up.

There is no better time than now to create a will, buy life or disability insurance, start an emergency fund, open your childrens' RESP, and start contributing to your own RRSP. It's time to examine your spending, identify your goals, and create a budget. Then stick to it!

Good parenting isn't about what you *buy* your children; it's about what you *give* them. Your children (or future children) are relying upon you to provide them with security and a happy household. How are the decisions you're making every day—large and small—meeting this need?

CHAPTER TWELVE

Learn More

Books and Print Resources

Argo, J.J. & Kelley J. Main, K.J. (2008). Stigma by Association in Coupon Redemption: Looking Cheap because of Others. in *Journal of Consumer Research* 35 (4):559–572.

Bach, D. (2008). *Go Green, Live Rich, Canadian Edition: 50 Simple Ways to Save the Earth (and Get Rich Trying)*. Scarborough, ON: Doubleday Canada.

———. (2006). *The Automatic Millionaire: Canadian Edition: A Powerful One-Step Plan to Live and Finish Rich*. Scarborough, ON: Doubleday Canada.

———. (2003) *Smart Couples Finish Rich, Canadian Edition: 9 Steps to Creating a Rich Future for You and Your Partner*. Toronto, ON: Doubleday Canada.

Baxter, A., Self, A., Dunsworth, K., Gunn, R. & Hanna, S. (2009). *Smart Cookies Guide to Making More Dough and Getting Out of Debt: How Five Young Women Got Smart, Formed a Money Group, and Took Control of Their Finances*. Toronto, ON: Vintage/Random House of Canada.

Bodnar, J. (2005). *Raising Money Smart Kids: What They Need to Know about Money and How to Tell Them*. Chicago, IL: Dearborn Trade Publishing/ Kaplan Professional Company.

Bradshaw, B. & Donaldson Bramley, L. (2010) The *Baby's Table: Over 150 Easy, Healthy and Homemade Recipes Your Baby Will Love*. Revised Edition. Toronto, ON: Random House of Canada.

Dacyczyn, A. (1998). *The Complete Tightwad Gazette: Promoting Thrift as a Viable Alternative Lifestyle*. New York, NY: Villard/Random House Publishing Group.

Deveau, S. (2003). *Sink or Swim: Get Your Degree Without Drowning in Debt.* Toronto, ON: Dundurn.

Editors of Reader's Digest. (2004). *Gifts for the Family: Over 120 Projects to Make for Those You Love in Under 30 Minutes.* Pleasantville, NY: Reader's Digest.

Ford, J. (2006). *Wonderful Ways to Love a Grandchild.* San Francisco, CA: Red Wheel/Weiser.

Foran, P. (2008). *The Smart Canadian's Guide to Saving Money: Pat Foran is On Your Side, Helping You to Stop Wasting Money, Start Saving It, and Build Your Wealth: Pat Foran is On Your Side, Helping You to Stop Wasting Money, Start Saving It, and Build Your Wealth,* 2nd ed. Toronto, ON: J. Wiley & Sons Canada.

Gerber, M.E. (1990). *The E-Myth: Why Most Small Businesses Don't Work and What to Do About It.* 2nd rev ed. Toronto, ON: HarperCollins Canada.

———. (2004). *The E-Myth Revisited: Why Most Small Businesses Don't Work and What to Do About It.* Revised Edition. New York, NY: HarperCollins.

Godfrey, J. (2003). *Raising Financially Fit Kids.* Berkeley, CA: Ten Speed Press.

Heintz, K. (2009). *Picky? Not Me, Mom!: A Parents' Guide to Children's Nutrition.* Calgary, AB: nutritionwithk.

Hewlett, S.A. (2002). *Creating a Life: Professional Women and the Quest for Children.* New York, NY: Talk Miramax Books/Hyperion.

Illsley Clarke, J., Dawson, C. & Bredehoft, D. (2003). *How Much Is Enough?: Everything You Need to Know to Steer Clear of Overindulgence and Raise Likeable, Responsible, and Respectful Children.* Cambridge, MA: Da Capo Press/Perseus Book Group

McGraw, S. (1994). *Gifts Kids Can Make.* Richmond Hill, ON: Firefly Books.

Myers, G. (2000). *Smart Mom's Babysitting Co-op Handbook.* Tacoma, WA: Tukwila Publishing.

Paré, J. (2001). *Gifts from the Kitchen.* Edmonton, AB: Company's Coming Publisher Ltd.

Richard, S. (2003). The *Healthy Family: Cooking For The Rushed.* North Salem, NY: Mint Publishers.

———. (2007). *Getting Ya Through the Summer: Cooking for the Rushed.* New York, NY: Scribner/Simon & Schuster.

———. (2007). *Life's on Fire: Cooking for the Rushed.* New York, NY: Scribner/Simon & Schuster.

———. (2007). *The Family Dinner Fix: Cooking for the Rushed.* New York, NY: Scribner/Simon & Schuster.

———. (2008) *Dinner Survival: The Most Uncomplicated, Approachable Way to Get Dinner to Fit Your Life.* New York, NY: Scribner/Simon & Schuster.

Ross, K. (2004). *Christmas Presents Kids Can Make.* Markham, ON: Fitzhenry & Whiteside.

Sinnema, J. (2005, September 11). Peer pressure pushes shoppers to pay premium. *The Calgary Herald*, p.A1.

Siemens, D., Thomas, L. & Smith, J. (2005). *The Big Cook.* Medicine Hat, AB: YouCan2Publishing.

Stanley, T.J. and Danko, W.D. (1996). *The Millionaire Next Door: The Surprising Secrets of America's Wealthy.* Atlanta, GA: Long Street Press.

Taylor, K. (2009). *397 Ways to Save Money: Spend Smarter & Live Well on Less.* Scarborough, ON: HarperCollins Canada.

Vaz-Oxlade, G. (1999). *A Woman of Independent Means: A Woman's Guide to Full Financial Security.* Toronto, ON: Stoddart Publishing.

———. (2009). *Debt-Free Forever: Take Control of Your Money and Your Life.* Scarborough, ON: HarperCollins Canada, Limited.

Weschler, T. (2006). *Taking Charge of Your Fertility, 10th Anniversary Edition: The Definitive Guide to Natural Birth Control, Pregnancy Achievement, and Reproductive Health.* New York, NY: Harper Paperbacks.

Winget, L. (2008). *You're Broke Because You Want to Be: How to Stop Getting By and Start Getting Ahead.* New York, NY: Gotham Books/Penguin Group.

Online Resources

American Society for Reproductive Medicine (2003). *Age and Fertility: A Guide for Patients.* Retrieved February 1, 2010 from <**http://www.asrm.org/Patients/patientbooklets/agefertility.pdf**>.

Beauchesne, E. (2008, November 5). *More Canadians expected to pass on RRSP contributions.* Retrieved February 1, 2010 from <**http://www.financialpost.com/personal-finance/rrsp/story.html?id=935658**>.

Bitti, M.T. (2005, August 20). Tuition savings very low: Poll finds RESPs unused. *National Post*, FW5.

CBC News. (2009, June 18). *Alberta minister apologizes to those offended by remarks on child-rearing.* Retrieved February 1, 2010 from <**http://www. cbc.ca/canada/edmonton/story/2009/06/18/edmonton-iris-evans-reaction.html**>.

Dorrell, K. (2004, September). Pregnancy: Bum Wrap: The Real Dirt on Diapers. *Today's Parent.* Retrieved February 1, 2010 from <**http://www. todaysparent.com/pregnancybirth/youandnewborn/article.jsp?conten t=20040730_130402_4732&page=2**>.

Environment Canada. (2004, August 5). What are the environmental benefits to using cloth versus disposable diapers? What types of cloth diapers are available? *Envirozine.* Retrieved February 1, 2010 from <**http://www.ec.gc. ca/envirozine/english/issues/45/any_questions_e.cfm**>.

Financial Consumer Agency of Canada. (2008). *Youth Financial Literacy Study.* Retrieved February 1, 2010 from <**http://www.fcac-acfc.gc.ca/eng/ publications/surveystudy/youthfinlit2008/youthfinlit2008_toc-eng. asp**>.

Hadzipetros, P. (2005, February 11). *Saving on your own.* CBC News. Retrieved February 1, 2010 from <**http://www.cbc.ca/news/background/ retirement/saving2.html**>.

Manitoba Agriculture, Food and Rural Initiatives. *The Costs of Raising Children.* Retrieved February 1, 2010 from <**http://home.gicable.com/~jqgregg/ Cost%20of%20raising%20children.pdf**>.

Mirowsky, J. (2004, August 14). *Age at First Birth, Health, and Mortality.* Paper presented at the annual meeting of the American Sociological Association. Retrieved February 1, 2010 from <**http://www.allacademic.com/meta/p_ mla_apa_research_citation/1/0/8/6/5/p108653_index.html**>.

Statistics Canada. (1997, November). *Failing Concerns: Business Bankruptcy in Canada.* Retrieved February 1, 2010 from <**http://dsp-psd.pwgsc.gc.ca/ Collection/Statcan/61-525-X/61-525-XIE1997001.pdf**>.

———. (1999, October 14). *The Daily. National Longitudinal Survey of Children and Youth: School Component.* Retrieved February 1, 2010 from <**www. statcan.gc.ca/daily-quotidien/991014/dq991014a-eng.htm**>.

———. (2006, December 7) *The Daily. 2005 Survey of Financial Security.* retrieved March 11, 2010 from <**www.statcan.gc.ca/daily-quotidien/ 061207/dq061207b-eng.htm**>.

The National Center on Addiction and Substance Abuse (CASA) at Columbia University. (2009, September). *The Importance of Family Dinners V.* Retrieved February 1, 2010 from <**http://casafamilyday.org/familyday/ files/media/Importance%20of%20Family%20Dinners%20V%209-18-09.pdf**>.

USC Education Savings Plans Inc. in Mississauga, Ontario, (2009, September) *2009 Guide to Education Costs in Canada.* Retrieved March 11, 2010 from <**http://www.usc.ca/public/csp/106/default.aspx**>.

Websites

- Adoption Council of Canada <**www.adoption.ca**>
- Advocis <**www.advocis.ca/consumers/designations/html**>
- Allrecipes.com <**www.allrecipes.com**>
- Big Cook <**www.thebigcook.com**>
- Big Oven <**www.bigoven.com**>
- Canada Education Savings Grant <**www.canlearn.ca**>
- Canada Revenue Agency <**www.cra-arc.gc.ca**>
- Canadian Finance Blog <**canadianfinanceblog.com/2009/10/13/how-much-does-raising-a-child-cost.htm**>
- Canadian Home Mortgage Corporation <**www.cmhc-schl.gc.ca**>
- Canadian Parents <**www.canadianparents.ca**>
- Connect Moms <**www.connectmoms.com**>
- Cooking for the Rushed <**www.cookingfortherushed.com**>
- Coupons <**www.coupons.com**>
- Diaper Making <**www.borntolove.com**>
- Download Budget Software <**www.download.com/**>
- Equifax Canada Inc. <**www.equifax.ca**>
- EnerGuide for Houses <**www.energuideforhouses.gc.ca/grant**>
- Enfamil First Connections <**www.enfamil.ca**>
- Freecycle Network™ <**www.freecycle.org**>
- Frugal for Life <**frugalforlife.blogspot.com**>
- Gail Vax-Oxlade <**www.Gailvazoxlade.com**>
- Geocaching: The Official Global GPS Cache Hunt Site <**www.geocaching.com**>

- Huggies <**www.huggies.com**>
- Industry Canada (Car Lease or Buy Calculator) <**www.ic.gc.ca**>
- Learning Disabilities Association of Canada <**www.ldac-acta.ca**>
- Make Your Own Sling <**www.wearsthebaby.com**>
  and <**www.mayawrap.com/n_sewsling.php**>
- Microsoft Corporation (Budgeting Templates) <**office.microsoft.com/en-us/default.aspx**>
- Multiple Births Canada <**www.multiplebirthscanada.org/english/index.php**>
- Nestle Baby Program <**www.nestle.ca**>
- Once a Month Mom <**www.onceamonthmom.com**>
- Pampers <**www.pampers.com**>
- Planning Family Vacations <**www.familytravelnetwork.com**>
- Safe Kids Canada <**www.safekidscanada.ca**>
- Save <**www.save.ca**>
- Savings: Frugal Living <**www.frugal.families.com/blog**>
- Service Canada (Canada Pension Plan Survivor Benefits) <**www.servicecanada.gc.ca/eng/isp/cpp/survivor.shtml**>
- Similac Advance Welcome Addition Club <**similac.ca/en/similac_welcome_addition_club/**>
- Smart Canucks <**smartcanucks.ca**>
- TFSA vs. RRSP calculator <**www.taxtips.ca/calculator/tfsavsrrsp.htm**>
- Save Money Blog <**www.savemoneyblog.net**>
- Today's Parent (Can You Afford to Stay Home? Calculator) <**www.todaysparent.ca**>
- Trans Union of Canada <**www.transunion.ca**>
- Vacation Rentals by Owner <**www.vrob.org**>
- Welcome Wagon <**www.welcomewagon.ca**>

Index